SCRAPBOOK

James Robert Parish

BALLANTINE BOOKS · NEW YORK

Picture Credits
NEA Service: pages 13, 23, 26
United Press Telephoto: pages 15, 29, 51 (bottom right), 53, 54, 56, 59, 64 (top left)
United Press Photo: pages 27 (left), 33, 51 (top)
UPI Telephoto: 60, 62 (top left), 64 (bottom left), 121, 123 (top right; bottom), 124, 153 (bottom)
Moss Photo Service: 63
UPI Photo: 65, 68, 72 (bottom), 154 (top right), 155
Bill Mark: 69
Las Vegas News Bureau: 83
Copyright © 1972 Metro-Goldwyn-Mayer, Inc.: 152
Wide World: 166, 170-175
NBC: 176

ISBN 0-345-27594-2

Manufactured in the United States of America

First Edition: October 1975
Sixth printing: October 1977

Design by Karin Batten & Elliot Kreloff

*For Elvis, the Colonel
and everyone who has cared about EP
over the years*

Acknowledgment:
Research Associate: Gregory Mank
Editor: T. Allan Taylor
Research Assistants: John Robert Cocchi;
Florence Solomon; Ted Albert; Nancy Barr;
Bruco Enterprises; Mrs. Loraine Burdick;
James Butler; Kingsley Canham; Maria
Columbus; Carol Coyne; Morris Everett, Jr.;
Film Fan Monthly, Film Favorites, (Charles
Smith); Sharon R. Fox; Pierre Guinle;
Mrs. R. F. Hastings; Richard Hudson;
Ginger Johnson; Ken D. Jones; Sandra
Lelyveld; Ernest Leogrande; Mr. & Mrs.
Hilton Levy; David McGillivray; Albert B.
Manski; Mrs. Earl Meisinger; Jim Meyer;
Peter Miglierini; Movie Poster Service
(Bob Smith); Movie Star News (Paula Klaw);
Fred A. Parish; Michael R. Pitts;
Quality First Photos; Nick Rosa; Sean Saver;
Lucy Smith; Don E. Stanke; Charles Stumpf;
Jeanne Tessum; Robert Vaubel;
Ann Whitley; Don Wigal

Special Acknowledgment:
Charlie Earle; Sharon R. Fox; Pierre Guinle;
Greg W. Mank; Mrs. Earl Meisinger; Peter
Miller; Nick Rosa; Florence Solomon;
Rich Wentzler

In Memphis, Tennessee, on a hot Saturday afternoon in the late summer of 1953, a dusty Ford pickup parks at the curb in front of the Memphis Recording Service, where, for four dollars, anyone who walks in off the street can make himself a phonograph record. The driver of the truck—an eighteen-year-old aspiring country-music singer who makes $40 a week as a deliveryman for an electrical-contracting company—has often before passed the Memphis Recording Service. But now he's saved up four dollars and has it in mind to make a record of his singing and guitar playing as a surprise birthday present for his mother. Toting a battered guitar, he climbs out of the truck and goes nervously into the office, where, in a soft-spoken, rural Mississippi accent, he politely inquires about making a record. He'll have to wait his turn, he's told, for there are a number of others ahead of him and there's only a single recording studio. So, he plumps down on a wooden chair next to the desk of the receptionist-office manager, a cheery woman in her thirties named Marion Keisker. Lean, six feet tall, the youthful delivery-truck driver has a puffy, pouty, and yet not unhandsome babyish face that is dominated by sullen, heavy-lidded blue eyes. He has on a long-sleeved pink shirt with its collar turned up at the neck, tight-fitting black trousers, and a pair of black motorcycle boots. But perhaps the most notable aspect of his appearance is his exceedingly long hair and heavy sideburns—naturally dark-blond hair that is so lacquered with greasy pomades that it appears almost to be jet black. He wears his pompadoured hair in a so-called duckass cut and at once reminds Miss Keisker of the sort of motorcycle tough played by Marlon Brando in *The Wild One*. But he is soft-spoken and polite almost to the point of being unctuous—a sheep in wolf's clothing.

While the young man quietly awaits his turn to record, Miss Keisker has a conversation with him that she often has occasion to remember years later. "What kind of singer are you?" she asks him. "I sing all kinds," he says. "Well, who do you sound like?" she asks. "I don't sound like nobody," he replies. "Do you sing hillbilly?" she asks. "Yeah, I sing hillbilly," he says. "Well, what hillbilly do you sound like?" she asks. "I don't sound like nobody," he says.

When it is at last the young man's turn to record, Miss Keisker goes back to the studio to help him get set up and ultimately stays to listen to him sing. For his first number, he sings "My Happiness," a song that has lately been made popular by the Ink Spots, and for the other side of the ten-inch acetate record he does a teary ballad entitled "That's When Your Heartache Begins." On both songs, he accompanies himself on the guitar, creating an effect that— as he himself years later recalled—sounds like "somebody beating on a bucket lid." Within ten minutes, he has made his record, paid his four dollars and left. But Miss Keisker, who'd at once been extraordinarily impressed by his unique singing style, has secretly put the last half of "My Happiness" and all of "That's When

Your Heartache Begins" on tape. And the following Monday morning, she gives the tape to her boss, Sam Phillips, who not only runs the Memphis Recording Service but is also the president of Sun Records, a small and struggling company that mainly puts out the records of black rhythm-and-blues singers. Phillips is as impressed with the young man's singing as Miss Keisker was. And so, although he doesn't yet know it, the young man's professional singing career has in a sense begun.

The summer of 1953. Eisenhower is President, Perry Como is the country's most popular singer, *I Love Lucy* is at the top of the TV ratings, and Norman Vincent Peale's *The Power of Positive Thinking* is a best-seller. A dull time in the history of America, to say the least, and a time, too, when most of the country's young are silent conformists in white-buck shoes and crewcuts. And so who could have dreamed that the young man who made his first record on that Saturday afternoon in Memphis would soon be one of the most influential national figures in changing the attitudes of America's young—to the point, in fact, where the *Sunday Times* of London would list him as one of "the shapers of the century"? Or who could have dreamed that within three years he'd be both the most famous and the highest-paid entertainer in the country? Or that he'd eventually star in thirty-one movies that would earn a worldwide total of more than $200 million? Or that, in 1975, he'd be getting $250,000 a week for performing in Las Vegas? Or that, finally, his records would sell in excess of 250 million copies—more records than the combined total sold of Bing Crosby, Frank Sinatra, and the Beatles? Who could have dreamed? Nobody. Least of all the young man himself, who was, of course, Elvis Aron Presley.

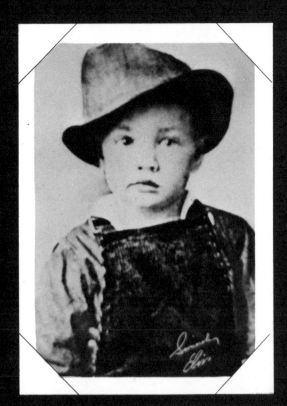

Elvis at age two

On 1935, Tupelo, Mississippi, pop. 6,000, was a rundown mill town in the middle of farm country in the northeastern corner of the state. It was the county seat of Lee County, and a couple of railroads ran through the town, but otherwise there was nothing in the least distinctive about Tupelo. And in the most depressed part of the town, East Tupelo, which was on the wrong side of the Mobile & Ohio Railroad tracks, a young couple named Gladys and Vernon Presley were then living on Old Saltillo Road in a two-room wood-frame house that was little more than a glorified shack. Gladys Presley, né Smith, was a $13-a-week sewing-machine operator for the Tupelo Garment Company, while Vernon Presley earned about an equal amount of money by working as a field hand on the farms around Tupelo. The Presleys were like figures out of one of Walker Evans'

PRESLEY BIRTHPLACE

Elvis Presley Youth Center and birthplace in Tupelo, Mississippi

Elvis, cowboy-style

When they'd married, in 1933, Vernon had been seventeen and Gladys, an older woman, had been twenty-one, and shortly after noon on January 8, 1935, their first child was born. A son. He was one of identical twin boys, the second of whom was born dead. And they named him Elvis Aron Presley, after no one in particular although Vernon's middle name was Elvis. Perhaps because the stillbirth of her second son had made her frightened for the life of her first

5

boy, Gladys Presley, who quit work in order to give her full attention to Elvis, brought him up as an extremely pampered and protected child. She rarely let him out of her sight to play with other children, for example, and she never went even down to the corner grocery store without Elvis in tow. Gladys Presley both doted on Elvis and spent endless hours teaching him to be well-behaved and polite—to always say "Yes, sir" and "Yes, ma'am" to his elders. And throughout the years of his childhood and youth Elvis was "a good boy" who never got into the slightest bit of trouble. It could even be said, in fact, that he was something of a mama's boy, for he doted on his mother as much as she doted on him.

While both Gladys and Vernon Presley could sing reasonably well, neither of them had any unusual talent for music. Nor was there a talent for music in either of their family backgrounds. (Their families, by the way, the Smiths and the Presleys, probably originally came to America from England, but no one knows for certain. "As far as I heard, us Presleys always come from around northeastern Mississippi, and so does the Smiths," Vernon Presley told an interviewer a few years ago.) From an early age, however, Elvis showed evidence of an exceptional singing talent. And by the time he was eight years old he was singing hymns with his mother and father at camp meetings, revivals, and at the Sunday-morning services of the First Assembly of God Church, which was one of the branches of a Pentecostal sect that the Presleys belonged to. When Elvis was ten years old, he entered a singing contest at the Lee County Fair, and won second prize—five dollars and a free admission to all the rides at the fair—for singing a maudlin song about a dog called "Old Shep."

When he was twelve years old, Elvis asked his parents for a bicycle, but they couldn't afford one. His mother, however, saved up some money and bought him a $12.95 guitar. At the time, he couldn't read music (and he still can't), and since there was no one around who could give him lessons on the guitar, he taught himself to play by listening to the radio and copying what he heard. A quiet, dreamy boy who had few friends, Elvis spent hour after hour listening to country music (i.e., hillbilly, as it used to be known) on the radio—to the records of Ernest Tubb, Roy Acuff, Jimmie Davis, and Jimmie Rodgers. And he also found himself peculiarly drawn to the music of such Negro blues singers as Booker White and B. B. King. Meanwhile, he continued to sing hymns at church. And he gradually developed a singing style that uniquely combined the sound of country music with that of Negro blues and old-time hymns. As he sang and played the guitar, he instinctively, too, began to move his body to the rhythm of the music in a way that imitated the twitching

*Elvis and senior prom date, with his
cousin, Gene Smith, and date*

ROTC member Elvis at Humes High School

and gyrating movements made by the hell-fire Pentecostal ministers who preached at the First Assembly of God Church. Thus, he learned naturally to move in a way that within a few years would earn him a nickname that he particularly hated—Elvis the Pelvis.

As a field hand and worker at odd jobs around Tupelo, Vernon Presley had never made much more than a marginal living for himself and his family. But then, in the late summer of 1948, he found himself at once out of work and totally broke. And so, in desperation, he piled his wife, his thirteen-year-old son, and all of their meager belongings into a broken-down 1939 Plymouth and moved to Memphis, Tennessee, which is a hundred miles northeast of Tupelo. In Memphis, Vernon landed a job as a $38.50-a-week laborer in a paint factory and the Presleys soon settled into a tiny apartment in a federally-sponsored low-income housing project known as Lauderdale Courts. And it was there that they lived until Elvis struck it rich in 1956 on a scale that no one could possibly have imagined.

In the fall of 1948, Elvis Aron Presley entered Humes High School, in Memphis, which had a student body of 1,600, or more pupils than there had been people in all of East Tupelo. Overwhelmed by the size of the school, and being anyway a basically shy and reticent country boy, Elvis made only a handful of friends at Humes. And, majoring in shop, he wasn't much of a student, either. Nor did he make any kind of a splash during his high-school years. In fact, he passed invisibly through four years at Humes with few of his teachers or classmates later being able to recall ever even having set eyes on him. In his one attempt to enter into the activities of the school, he went out for the football team, but, weighing only 150 pounds at the time, he proved to be too light to make the varsity. And so, to his bitter disappointment, he was forced to quit the team.

Perhaps the only distinctive thing about Elvis during his high-school years was that he had long hair and heavy sideburns when just about all the rest of his classmates wore crewcuts. (Presley later explained that he wore his hair long in high school because he dreamed of being a motorcycler and also because, baby-faced, he wanted to make himself look older.) And he dressed differently from his classmates, too, in flaming-pink shirts, pink-and-black sports jackets, black pegged pants, and white shoes. Clearly, although shy, he had a deep yearning to be the center of attraction. But only once in his high-school years did he gain any special attention. In his senior year, he reluctantly agreed to play his guitar and sing in an all-school variety show that was put on before the entire student body of 1,600. More than thirty students performed in the show, but only Elvis —greeted after his song by a storm of cheers and applause—was called back on stage to do an encore. "They liked me," he said dazedly, with tears in his eyes as he came off stage after his encore, "they really liked me."

The Elvis D.A. and roll collar

Early publicity pose

10

On the club circuit, 1955

Of course, Elvis never for a moment considered going on to college, and for months before he'd been graduated from Humes High School, in June, 1953, he had a full-time ushering job in a downtown Memphis movie theater. And he soon moved on from ushering to work briefly as a factory hand for the Precision Tool Company. After which, in late July of 1953, he landed the truck-driving job (with the Crown Electric Company) that he was holding down when he made his four-dollar record at the Memphis Recording Service. At the age of eighteen, he dreamed of someday becoming a country-music singer, but he nonetheless sensibly covered his bets by enrolling in a night school, where he studied to become an electrician. At the time, Vernon Presley was earning some $2,000 a year as a laborer in the paint factory, and Elvis was determined that he wasn't going to wind up like his father. As an electrician, he reckoned, he'd at least have a profession for himself.

As noted, Sam Phillips was extremely impressed by the tape that he heard of Presley singing. Still, he was then working night and day to make a go of Sun Records, and he didn't get around to calling Elvis for months, even though Marion Keisker kept reminding him of "the kid with the long hair." And even after calling Presley to his office and listening to him sing in person, Phillips wasn't convinced that Elvis was yet ready to record professionally. Instead, he put Elvis in touch with Scotty Moore, a twenty-one-year-old guitar player, and Bill Black, a twenty-three-year-old bass player, and suggested that the three of them get together and see if they could work up a few songs to record. And for several months in the late winter and early spring of 1954, Presley, Moore, and Black met almost every night to play blues and country music. Finally, in June, they went back to Phillips and said that they were ready to record. Phillips listened to them play for a few minutes and agreed. Thus, in the tiny Sun Records studio at 706 Union Street on a night in the late June of 1954, Elvis Presley, backed by Moore on the guitar and Black on the bass, made his first professional recording. For the A side of the record, he sang "That's All Right, Mama," a song that had originally been written and recorded in the 1940s by Arthur "Big Boy" Crudup, a black blues singer whom Elvis had listened to on the radio for years. And then, for the B, or flip, side of the record, he did "Blue Moon of Kentucky," a bluegrass country-music song that had been made famous years earlier by Bill Monroe. The record of "That's All Right, Mama" and "Blue Moon of Kentucky" wasn't destined to be Number 1 on the charts or to sell a million copies, as so many of Elvis's later records did, but it was nonetheless a minor landmark in the annals of American popular music. Not only because it was Elvis Presley's first record, but also because it was the first record to combine the sound of white hillbilly music with the sound of Negro blues to form a unique new sound that would soon come to be known as "rockabilly."

Sam Phillips released "That's All Right, Mama" (perhaps a psychologically interesting title for the first song to be recorded by a young man with a galloping Oedipus complex) in August, 1954. To help promote the record, he took it around to Dewey Phillips (no relation), who was then one of the top disc jockeys at WHBQ

in Memphis. Dewey Phillips agreed to play the record on a program called *Red, Hot and Blue,* and on the night that it was scheduled to be aired for the first time Elvis turned on the family radio at home to WHBQ for the benefit of his parents. But then, too nervous himself to listen, he went off to see a Tony Curtis movie. About halfway through the picture, however, his mother and father came breathlessly into the theater looking for him. Dewey Phillips had played "That's All Right, Mama" fourteen times in a row and the record was causing a sensation all over Memphis—scores of listeners had called the station to praise it and now Phillips wanted Elvis down at WHBQ to be interviewed on the air. Elvis bolted excitedly from the theater and ran all the way downtown to the WHBQ studios. At the station, he nervously told Phillips that he "didn't know nothin' about bein' interviewed." "Just don't say nothing dirty," said Phillips, and then, supposedly as preparation for the on-the-air interview, he proceeded to ask Elvis a number of questions about himself. Which he calmly and coolly answered. But what Elvis didn't know was that the microphone was already on while he was talking. "So, when's the interview start, Mr. Phillips?" asked Elvis. "It's already over, boy," said Phillips.

With Dewey Phillips, at WHBQ studios, Memphis, the first disc jockey to broadcast Elvis' recording of "That's All Right Mama"

The 1956 Elvis—ready for success

Elvis's record of "That's All Right, Mama" sold around 20,000 copies, got as high as third on the Memphis country-and-western sales charts, and even received national attention in *Billboard,* which described Presley as "a potent new chanter who can sock over a tune for either the country or r & b markets." Moreover, the record led to appearances by Elvis and his two back-up men on a number of country-music radio programs, including *Grand Ole Opry* and *Louisiana Hayride,* and also to invitations to appear in person at county fairs, schools, and small-town auditoriums. So, Presley quit his truck-driving job and chipped in with Moore and Black to buy a 1954 Chevrolet Bel Air. And off they went on the country-music tour to cash in on the success of their record.

It was while appearing on stage for the first time on that tour in obscure southern towns throughout Tennessee, Alabama, and Florida that Elvis first discovered that the twitching and

Elvis' first nationwide TV appearance, January 28, 1956, with the Dorsey Brothers on Stage Show

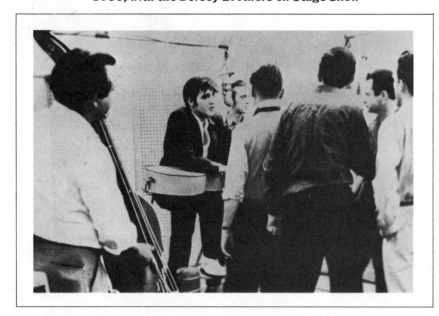

Gettin' it together at a 1956 RCA record session

gyrating he did while singing had a highly unusual effect on his audience. And especially on the teen-age girls in the audience. That is, his at first unconscious suggestive movements while doing a number like "Good Rockin' Tonight" turned them into screaming hysterics, of a type not seen in America since the squealing bobby-soxers who swooned over Frank Sinatra in the early 1940s. Before long, too, riots began to break out in the audience wherever Presley appeared.

As word of Presley's astonishing ability to turn on audiences spread through the country-music world in late 1954 and early 1955 he was soon booked into theaters and ball parks in cities like Jacksonville, Nashville, and his home town of Memphis. At first, he appeared on the lower half of a bill headed by country-music star Hank Snow, but he soon became the star of his own touring show. More and more riots broke out. In Jacksonville, for instance, a platoon of cops had to fight off a shrieking horde of teen-

Memphis, July 5, 1956: the Mr. Dynamite—Elvis Presley—demonstration at Russwood Park charity benefit

age girls who were battling to get up on stage in order to at least touch Elvis and maybe even to tear off a piece of his pink sports jacket.

Meanwhile, Presley made more records for Sam Phillips at Sun, with whom he'd now signed a long-term contract. In October, 1954, he made his second record, "Good Rockin' Tonight," which was slightly less successful than "That's All Right, Mama." In the first months of 1955, however, he recorded "Milkcow Blues Boogie," "I'm Left, You're Right, She's Gone," and "Mystery Train," and all three were smash country-music hits, if virtually unheard of outside the South.

From his records and public appearances, Presley suddenly found himself making more money than he'd ever dreamed of. And he spent it on a brand-new 1955 pink Cadillac and on setting himself and his parents up in a $40,000 ranch house in one of Memphis's more elegant neighborhoods. But the money he was then earning, some $2,000 a week, was only a hint of what he'd soon be making.

By the early fall of 1955, Presley had acquired a personal manager (a Memphis disc jockey named Bob Neal) and been voted "the most promising new country performer of the year" in a poll taken by *Billboard*; he'd also caught the attention far away in New York of RCA Victor Records. Indeed, in the person of Steven Sholes, who was the head of artist-and-

repertoire of the country-music division in Nashville, RCA moved in to buy out Presley's contract with Sun Records and take over the management of his recording activities. Before Sholes could sign Elvis with RCA, however, another party maneuvered himself shrewdly into the picture. A man who was to become the most important person in Presley's life aside from his mother. And he was, of course, the now legendary Colonel Tom Parker.

On 1955, Colonel Tom Parker — whose field-grade military rank was strictly an honorary one conferred on him in 1953 by Tennessee's Governor Frank G. Clements—was plump, waddling, and forty-five, a balding press agent, promoter, and manager of country-music singers who reminded more than one observer of a real-life counterpart of the sort of down-at-the-heels entrepreneurs played by W. C. Fields in movies like *Poppy* and *You Can't Cheat an Honest Man*. Colonel Parker, for example, was alleged to have once caught a flock of sparrows, spray-painted them yellow, and sold them as canaries. And he was also supposedly the creator of a carnival sideshow attraction known as the Dancing Chickens—under a bed of wet straw in a henhouse he'd placed an elec-

In Las Vegas, 1956

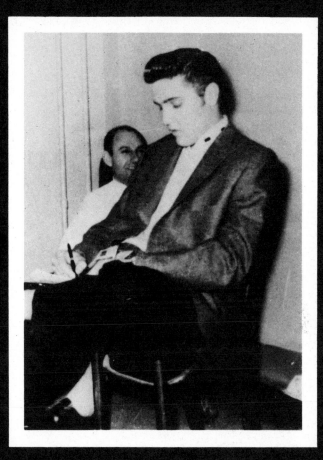

Backstage at Municipal Auditorium in San Antonio, waiting to go on

With "Uncle Miltie" on the Milton Berle Show, April 1956

Rehearsing for show with Steve Allen

Performing as usual

Elvis knockin' 'em dead in Fort Worth, Texas

"Weeelll Since Ma Baby Left Me"

tric hot plate, which, when switched on, caused the chickens to do something akin to the Charleston.

The Colonel was the son of carnival performers who died before he was ten years old. Taken in by an uncle who was also in the carnival business, he spent his childhood and youth working in various touring carnivals and small-time circuses all over the South. A short-order cook, a roustabout, he did everything—from selling hotdogs to reading palms to being the front man for a pony-and-monkey act. In the late 1930s, he'd married and given up the traveling life to settle down in Tampa, Florida, where he promoted country-music shows and so got to be chummy with such hillbilly stars as Minnie Pearl and Roy Acuff. Friendships which led to a job, back on the road, as an advance man for a touring show headed by Eddy Arnold, who in the early 1940s was one of the rising stars of the country-music world. And the Colonel proved to be such a successful advance man that he was soon promoted to Arnold's personal manager. In 1944, Parker negotiated a

Elvis does a Marlon Brando, Wild Ones style

recording contract for Arnold with RCA Victor, and a number of Arnold's records for RCA became major hits, including "Bouquet of Roses," which sold more than a million copies in 1947 and made Arnold the reigning king of country music.

In the early 1950s, after they'd been together for almost ten years, Parker and Eddy Arnold had a falling out, the upshot of which was that the Colonel found himself out of a job. After a couple of lean years, the Colonel landed on his feet again, hooking on as personal manager to Hank Snow, who by 1954 had replaced Eddy Arnold as the Number 1 singing star of country music. In the spring of 1955, when Elvis Presley joined the Hank Snow Jamboree for a ten-day tour of Texas, the Colonel had the opportunity to watch him perform show after show. And he quickly recognized the fact that Elvis had the potential to become an even bigger star than either Eddy Arnold or Hank Snow. He immediately wanted to become Elvis's personal manager, but Elvis already had a personal manager, of course, Bob Neal. Still, the Colonel recognized the fact, as apparently no one else had, that the way to Elvis Presley's heart was through Elvis Presley's mother. And so, whenever he was in Memphis, the Colonel took to making social calls on Mr. and Mrs. Presley in their new home, gallantly bringing flowers to Gladys Presley and impressing both parents with W. C. Fields-like flattery. Within a few weeks, he'd persuaded them that there was only one man in all of America who was qualified to guide their son's rising career. And that man, of course, was Colonel Tom Parker. He worked his wiles, too, directly on Elvis, and in November, 1955, at the urging of his mother, Elvis ditched Bob Neal and signed up with Colonel Parker. The terms of their agreement have always remained secret, but it is known that the Colonel cut himself in for at least 25 per cent of Elvis and that the figure may even be a good deal higher. Elvis also agreed to place himself entirely in the Colonel's hands—to leave all of the decisions about his career entirely up to Parker. And Elvis has done so right up to this day. For twenty years now,

Colonel Tom Parker has been 100 per cent in charge of Elvis Presley.

Of course, as a man who could foist off sparrows on the public as canaries and make chickens dance, the Colonel was eminently qualified to peddle Elvis Presley to the American people. Besides, to be perfectly serious, Colonel Parker had high-level connections in the country-music world and with companies like RCA Victor, connections that Memphis small-timers like Sam Phillips and Bob Neal simply didn't have. And Elvis was indeed in just about the best possible managerial hands. Now, with Colonel Tom Parker sturdily at the helm, Elvis's career, as 1956 began, was about to go through the roof.

F orget about Eisenhower's landslide defeat of Adlai Stevenson for the second time. Or the Suez crisis. Or even Marilyn Monroe's marriage to Arthur Miller. Nineteen fifty-six in America was the year of Elvis Presley. And no one else.

Before the year had begun, Colonel Parker had made a deal for Presley with RCA Victor Records whereby RCA bought out Elvis's contract with Sam Phillips and Sun Records for $35,000. And beginning in January, 1956, with "Heartbreak Hotel," one after another of Elvis's RCA releases not only became Number 1 on the charts in America but also sold more than a million copies. Among his incredible string of hits in 1956 were "Hound Dog" and "Don't Be Cruel," which were both at different times Number 1 in the country even though they were two sides of the same record—something that had never happened before and has never happened since. And in 1956 Presley also had Number 1 hits and million-copy sellers with "Tutti Frutti," "Money Honey," "Shake, Rattle and Roll," "Love Me Tender," and "Blue Suede Shoes."

In 1956, too, Presley symbolically stomped with his blue suede shoes all over Pat Boone's

"You Ain't Nothin' But a Hounddog"

With Richard Egan and Debra Paget in Love Me Tender

With Mildred Dunnock and Debra Paget in Love Me Tender

Publicity pose for Love Me Tender

On the set of Love Me Tender with Debra Paget

With William Campbell, Mildred Dunnock, and Richard Egan in Love Me Tender

20th Century-Fox presents
RICHARD EGAN · DEBRA PAGET
and introducing
ELVIS PRESLEY
in his first motion picture
LOVE ME TENDER
MR. ROCK 'N' ROLL IN THE STORY HE WAS BORN TO PLAY!
CINEMASCOPE
CO-STARRING
ROBERT MIDDLETON · WILLIAM CAMPBELL · NEVILLE BRAND
with MILDRED DUNNOCK · BRUCE BENNETT
PRODUCED BY DAVID WEISBART
DIRECTED BY ROBERT D. WEBB
SCREENPLAY BY ROBERT BUCKNER
BASED ON A STORY BY MAURICE GERAGHTY
Copyright 1956 20th Century-Fox Film Corp.
COUNTRY OF ORIGIN U. S. A.
Property of National Screen Service Corp. Licensed for display only in connection with the exhibition of this picture at your theatre. Must be returned immediately thereafter.

Lookin' very cool for 1956

"Presley for President" fans at Los Angeles Airport, 1956. Elvis had just arrived to make his first movie, Love Me Tender

Elvis in pensive mood

white bucks and all that they represented. Low-down, raucous, and even explicitly sexual (e.g., "Good Rockin' Tonight" was not only about dancing), Presley's new rockability sound was running roughshod over the saccharine sound of songs like "Love Letters in the Sand." And maybe especially because their uptight parents were horrified by Elvis, America's teen-agers went wild for him and his music. For the first time, they had a music that was distinctively their own, with a beat and lyrics that reflected their yearnings for rebellion against the puritan and sterile adult world of Eisenhower, Levit-towns, *Make Room for Daddy*, Eddie Fisher, Jo Stafford, Wonder bread, and the Edsel. In a sense, too, Elvis paved the way for Bob Dylan, for the Beatles, for long hair, for the sexual revolution, for the rise of the counterculture, and for all of the other revolutionary changes in life style that American youth brought about in the 1960s. But, of course, he did it inadvertently. All Elvis wanted to do was sing and make as much money as possible. For no one could be less politically conscious or socially aware than Elvis Presley.

Inevitably, as one Presley record after another reached the top of the charts, Elvis began to get offers to appear on television. And Colonel Parker eagerly snapped them up—for increasingly higher amounts of money. Presley made his first nationwide TV appearance in January, 1956, on Tommy and Jimmy Dorsey's Saturday night CBS *Stage Show* program, for a fee of $1,250. And he later returned to make five further appearances on *Stage Show*. In the spring of that year, he was twice a guest on the *Milton Berle Show*, for $5,000 each time. And that summer he was paid $7,500 for a single appearance on the *Steve Allen Show*.

Accustomed to singers like Perry Como and

sing Crosby, American TV viewers had never seen anything like greasy-haired Elvis with his sideburns and duckass cut. Typically, he appeared on TV wearing tight-fitting, pink-striped black pants, a pink shirt with its collar turned up, and a drape-shaped pink sports jacket. And then, with his guitar slung low around his neck and his legs spread wide apart, he'd snap his right knee as he launched into a song—"Wellll, since mah bayy-beee left me/Ah've found a new place to dwell/It's down at the end of Lonely Street/It's Heartbreak Hotel." As he sang, he twitched both legs while undulating his pelvis in a manner that had previously been associated only with burlesque strippers. In other words, on nationwide TV he appeared to be imitating the movements of sexual intercourse (in Newsweek, John Lardner described him as looking like "a lovesick outboard motor"), and while teen-age girls across America were evidently all out having orgasms while watching Elvis, their parents were having conniptions. Indeed, a storm of anti-Elvis sentiment was soon sweeping America. Women's groups, PTAs, Catholic priests, rabbis, ministers (including Billy Graham), and political leaders angrily spoke out against Elvis and attempted both to have him kept off TV and to have his records banned from radio. "Appalling taste," said an outraged editorial in the New York Times, while a leading Catholic magazine, America, urged that the TV networks be forced to "stop showing such nauseating stuff." And the TV critics—most of whom, of course, knew absolutely nothing about country music—damned him as a totally untalented performer. "Mr. Presley has no discernible singing ability," wrote Jack Gould in

the New York Times, and other critics were equally harsh on him.

In 1956, the highest-rated variety show on American television was Ed Sullivan's Toast of the Town, which was on for an hour on CBS every Sunday evening at eight o'clock. In those days, all of America watched Ed Sullivan on Sunday evening. When Presley had made his first appearances on TV, Sullivan, who was both politically conservative and a devout Catholic, had publicly said that under no circumstances would he ever have Elvis on his program. By the late summer of 1956, however, Presley was without doubt the biggest single attraction in American show business. And so Sullivan, who was above all interested in high ratings for his Toast of the Town, swallowed his pride and got on the phone to Colonel Tom Parker. Gleefully the Colonel held Sullivan up for the highest pay that any TV guest had ever received—$50,000 for three appearances. Thus, on the night of Sunday, September 9, 1956, Elvis Presley appeared on Ed Sullivan's show. But Ed Sullivan didn't. He somehow couldn't make it that evening and was replaced at the last minute by the British actor Charles Laughton. Elvis's two songs in the show were broadcast as a live insert from the CBS studios in Hollywood, but as an indicator of exactly how uptight America was that year, Presley was seen—per the network censor's explicit instructions—only from the waist up. Still, even though America wasn't permitted to view his gyrating lower half, Presley's appearance on Toast of the Town gave the program the highest ratings in its history—an unbelievable 82.6 per cent of the TV audience, a percentage that in those days translated into

Christmas, 1956, in Memphis, with his parents and Las Vegas showgirl Dorothy Harmony

appearances on the show got it almost equally high ratings. Whether Billy Graham, Ed Sullivan, and others liked it or not, Presley was now ensconced at the top of the heap—the Number . entertainer in America.

Even before Ed Sullivan had signed up Presley, Hollywood had been after him. In fact, he made his first appearance on *Toast of the Town* from Hollywood because he was out there making his first movie, *Love Me Tender*, which was part of a $450,000 three-picture deal that Colonel Parker had negotiated for him with Twentieth Century-Fox. *Love Me Tender* was a Civil War story about the rivalry of two Southern brothers for the love of the same woman into which four songs and a death scene by Elvis were sandwiched. When the picture opened, in November, 1956, both it and Elvis were unmercifully panned by the critics. *Time* magazine, for example, described Elvis as looking like a cross between a sausage and a Walt Disney goldfish and as having about the same acting talent as a sausage. But the picture nonetheless packed them in all over the country and within weeks it had earned a profit of more than $2 million.

By the time that Elvis began his third movie, *Jailhouse Rock*, in the fall of 1957, the Colonel had upped his price to $250,000 per picture, *plus* 50 per cent of the profits. And by the middle of the 1960s Elvis was getting $750,000 per picture, again *plus* 50 per cent of the profits. In all, from 1956 to 1969, Elvis made thirty-one feature films, most of which were fairly inane musicals set in places like Hawaii, Acapulco, and Las Vegas, in which he starred as, say, a sensitive but misunderstood singing racing-car driver or a sensitive but misunderstood singing prize fighter who for some reason is constantly surrounded by a bevy of bikini-clad starlets. Still, the pictures, which did particularly well in rural areas, at drive-ins, and overseas, grossed a worldwide total of over $200 million and earned Elvis and the Colonel perhaps $25 million as their share of the profits.

After finishing *Love Me Tender*, Elvis topped

on 1956 by making a nationwide singing tour during which he was paid as much as $25,000 for a one-night stand in a big-city auditorium or a ball park. And everywhere that he appeared in the fall of that year there were highly publicized riots of screaming and fainting teen-age girls. Followed by damning newspaper editorials and anti-Elvis magazine articles. America's love-hate relationship with Elvis Presley had become a kind of nationwide obsession.

Before going off on the tour with Elvis, Colonel Tom Parker had stocked up on thousands of eight-by-ten glossy photographs of Presley that he'd bought wholesale for five cents each. And now, wearing a change apron, the Colonel could be found in the lobby before and after each of Elvis's performances hustling the photographs at fifty cents each. Even though his cut of the receipts for the evening might be as high as $10,000, the Colonel simply couldn't resist the opportunity to make himself a fast extra buck.

While Elvis was earning millions in 1956 from his records, his TV appearances, his movie deals, and his personal appearances, the Colonel, in partnership with a merchandising expert named Hank Saperstein, had also shrewdly got Presley into the business of endorsing products with his name attached to them. And as the Elvis Presley industry boomed across America in late 1956, teen-agers were paying millions for Elvis Presley T shirts, sneakers, charm bracelets, stuffed hound dogs, perfume, lipsticks (in such shades as Hound Dog Orange and Heartbreak Hotel Orange), and two-dollar plaster-of-Paris busts of guess who. And Elvis's share of the take from the products, at an average of 6 per cent of the gross, amounted to around $600,000. Which, of course, was merely icing on the cake of an income for Elvis that in 1956 probably amounted to close to $10 million. Nineteen fifty-six. For Elvis Presley, it was a very good year.

nd then came 1957. Once again, Elvis had an almost unbelievable string of Number 1 records that sold a million or more copies. Among them were "All Shook Up," "Teddy Bear," "Loving You," and "Jailhouse Rock." By 1957, too, RCA had issued two albums of his songs, and those albums became the first in history to sell more than a million copies. He also made a pair of highly successful movies—*Loving You* and *Jailhouse Rock*—in 1957, and he continued throughout the year to tour when not making pictures. And the Elvis Presley industry—a line of products to which stuffed Teddy bears, paper dolls, and coloring books had now been added—went on booming. And so Elvis probably earned as much in 1957 as he had in 1956.

By the middle of 1957, Elvis's biggest problem was to find ways to spend all the money he was earning. In July, 1957, he bought a $100,000 estate named Graceland on the outskirts of Memphis. The Graceland mansion was

That Presley smile

fronted by white colonial pillars, had twenty-three rooms, and stood on a hilltop amid thirteen acres of private lawns. To keep out the hordes of clamoring teen-age girls who now turned up wherever he was, Elvis had a ten-foot-high fence built around Graceland. And he also put in an enormous swimming pool. Moreover, he had the interior of the mansion redecorated to include mirrored bedrooms with midnight-blue walls, a motion-picture screening room, and an outsize playroom in which there was a pool table, a jukebox, a soda fountain (Elvis is a lifelong teetotaler who never drinks anything

In Memphis with Hollywood starlet Yvonne Lime, April 1957

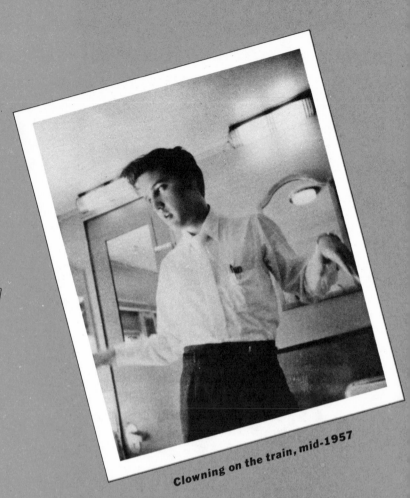

Clowning on the train, mid-1957

Quiet moment on the road

A cool dip

Rehearsal time

Won't you be——my Teddy bear

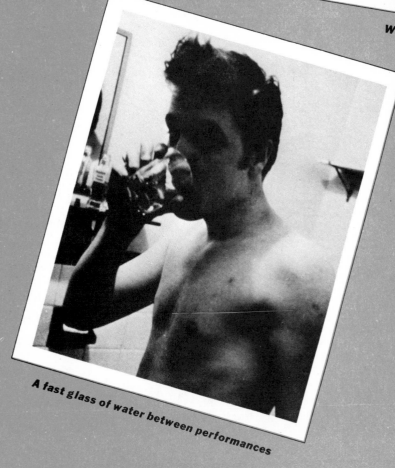

A fast glass of water between performances

35

On location with
Dolores Hart for
Loving You

Publicity pose with
Lizabeth Scott for
Loving You

Promotional item for Loving You

ELVIS PRESLEY
EXCLUSIVE R C A VICTOR RECORDING STAR
Loving You CHARM BRACELET
COPYRIGHT 1956 ELVIS PRESLEY ENTERPRISES ALL RIGHTS RESERVED

*The star
of* Loving You

*With Dolores Hart,
Lizabeth Scott, and
Wendell Corey in*
Loving You

In Loving You
(1957)

*A pre-recording ses-
sion for* Loving You
*with composer-
conductor Walter
Scharf (left) and
dance director
Charles O'Curran*

Lovin' 'em tender at a March 1957 performance in Fort Wayne, Indiana

stronger than ice-cream sodas and Pepsi-Cola), a piano, a couple of color TVs, and an expensive layout of stereo equipment.

And into Graceland he moved his mother and father, of course, plus his grandmother, an aunt, two uncles, and assorted other relatives. But perhaps the most talked-about group to take up residence at Graceland was a platoon of his old buddies from high school who soon came to be known as the Memphis Mafia. In their hairstyles and dress, the eight or so members of the Memphis Mafia closely modeled themselves after Elvis. And everywhere he went in 1957, from Graceland to Hollywood, Las Vegas, and the cities that he hit on tour, they lived and traveled with him. Each of them—"good ole boys" with

The audience

With Natalie Wood in Hollywood, 1957

Back to the grind

Elvis in action in Jailhouse Rock

Advertisement for Jailhouse Rock (1957)

With Judy Tyler in
Jailhouse Rock

With William Forrest
and Jennifer Holden
in Jailhouse Rock

Elvis Presley

Backstage at October 1957 San Francisco concert

Mrs. Presley and Elvis' one-time romantic interest Barbara Hearn backstage at Tupelo Fair

44

In 1957

names like Bobby "Red" West, Charlie Hodge, and Lamar Fike—was paid a salary of a couple of hundred dollars a week. For which they served as Elvis's personal squad of bodyguards as well as his chauffeurs, dressers, and errand runners. But he mainly kept them around in order to have resident playmates for the fun and games that he enjoyed when not working. They played touch football with him, for example, raced slot cars, flew model airplanes, and gunned motorcycles around the grounds at Graceland. On one occasion, Elvis and his live-in buddies bought out the entire stock of flashbulbs from every camera store in Memphis, threw them into the swimming pool, and then proceeded to make a day-and night-long game of shooting the flashbulbs in the pool with BB guns. "What Elvis liked was that there explodin' sound when you hit one of them flashbulbs with a BB—he'd laugh like a son-of-a-bitch," one of the participants in the flashbulb-shooting game later explained.

At Graceland, and at whatever Bel Air mansion he rented when in Los Angeles to make a movie, there was always a round-the-clock party going on. At the parties, Elvis, his buddies, and an endless succession of pretty girls sat around drinking Pepsi-Cola, watching TV, joshing, listening to records, dancing, and from time to time splitting off to bedrooms for rounds of sex. The girls—many of whom were recruited from

The pre-Graceland Elvis home, 1957

**With Carolyn Jones
and Walter Matthau
in King Creole
(1958)**

In King Creole

10216-20

KING CREOLE

With Dolores Hart in King Creole

With Carolyn Jones in King Creole

Elvis and friends

Portrait of an American Idol, painting by Italian primitive, Oscar De Mejo. The late actor James Dean is represented at upper left.

Inspecting new wrought-iron gates at his Graceland home in Memphis

Elvis and guest Venetia Stevenson, Hollywood actress, in Memphis, 1957

With stripper Tempest Storm in Las Vegas, 1957

among the throngs of teen-agers who hung around night and day outside the gates of Graceland or at the doorstep of his rented Bel Air mansion—had one main object in mind: to go to bed with Elvis Presley. And there is every evidence that a considerable number of them suc-ceeded, although most of them ended up being bedded down by one or another or all of the members of the Memphis Mafia. Or so claimed the Memphis Mafia.

By 1957, Presley had become so famous that it was no longer possible for him to go anywhere without being mobbed by his teen-age fans. So, when at Graceland, he took to renting a Memphis amusement park at night after it had closed to the public. With his buddies, plus whatever girls chanced to be on hand, Elvis would ride on the amusement park rides from midnight until dawn. His favorite was the Dodge 'Em cars, in which he and his friends would cheerfully scoot about for hours in the vast and otherwise deserted park. And he'd sometimes, too, rent movie theaters and roller-skating rinks for the night. In those days, Elvis Presley was essentially still an adolescent, with the emotional maturity of a thirteen-year-old boy.

As the money rolled in, Elvis spent tens of thousands of dollars on clothes, including a $10,000 gold suit. But his biggest expenditure was on cars, as he took to buying Cadillacs, Lincoln Continentals, and Rolls-Royces as casually as most men buy neckties. He also bought a small fleet of foreign sports cars, limousines, buses, pickup trucks, motorcycles, and go-Karts. On one occasion, he bought seven brand-new tractors on which he and the members of the Memphis Mafia staged races around Graceland. The result was that a number of the tractors were wrecked and lawns were torn up all over the estate.

Elvis obviously had far more cars than he possibly had any need for. They were parked all over Graceland, unused and virtually brand new, to be either sold or given away when Elvis had grown bored with having them around. More than once, the story has been told of a friend or even a stranger who admired one of Elvis's expensive cars and suddenly found himself the owner of it. "Hey, that's a beautiful Jaguar," someone might say to Elvis. "You really like it?" Elvis would ask. "Yeah!" "You got a dollar?" "Uh-huh." "Sold—it's yours!" And so went life for Presley in 1957—getting, spending, and giving away.

Army physician Capt. Leonard Glick giving Elvis his preinduction physical in Memphis, January 1957

$\bigcirc$n early 1958, shortly after he'd finished making his fourth movie, *King Creole*, something rather startling happened to Elvis Presley—he got drafted into the United States Army. For two years. And so, from an income of around $400,000 a month, he abruptly dropped down to a private's salary of $78 a month. Although, of course, the royalties from his records and the profits from his movies continued to pour in. Also, he'd recorded a backlog of songs to be released while he was away in the Army so that the record-buying public wouldn't forget who he was. Colonel Tom Parker, too, was laboring mightily on the home front to make certain that Elvis wouldn't be forgotten. "I consider it my patriotic duty," said the Colonel, "to keep Elvis in the ninety-per-cent tax bracket while he's in the Army." Still, there were many of his detractors who believed that when Elvis entered the Army, on March 24, 1958, his career—thank God—was over. Presley, they claimed, was a faddish figure who would be all but forgotten in

United States Army swearing-in, Memphis, March 24, 1958

two years. This turned out to be wishful thinking on their part, however, for Elvis's popularity scarcely diminished at all during his military service.

On the advice of Colonel Parker, Elvis chose not to become an entertainer in the Army's Special Services as the Pentagon had hoped he'd be—but instead to be simply a regular soldier. And so, along with a bunch of other recruits, he was sent first to Fort Chaffee, Arkansas, where the most publicized haircut of 1958 took place —Elvis's long hair and sideburns were shorn off with electric clippers. And, sporting a crewcut, off he went to Fort Hood, Texas, for eight weeks of basic training.

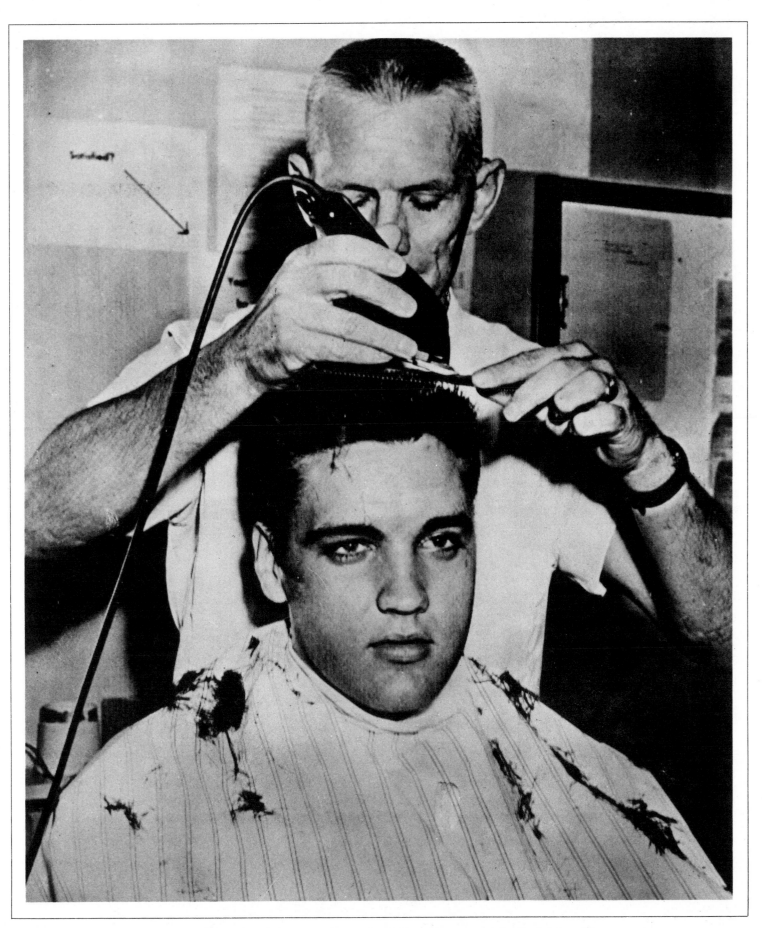

The famous Presley D.A. gives way to regulation Army crewcut, administered by James Peterson at Fort Chaffee, Arkansas, March 25, 1958

Sfc. Calvin Rhoades giving Asiatic flu shot to Private Elvis, March 26, 1958

After basic and a seven-day leave back home at Graceland, Elvis returned to Fort Hood to undergo eight weeks of armored training, and it was then that something genuinely tragic happened to Elvis for perhaps the first time in his life: his mother died.

For a long time, Gladys Presley, who was forty-six when she died, on August 14, 1958,

had been seriously overweight. And, especially in front of her famous son, she'd been desperately ashamed of it. So she'd got herself some diet pills, which were actually amphetamines, and mixed them with the enormous amount of alcohol that she'd been downing in her depression over being fat. The official cause of her death was given as a heart attack, but it's highly

Elvis battling his duffel bag at Fort Chaffee, March 31, 1958

A slim and trim Elvis boards Navy transport in Brooklyn for European duty, September 22, 1958

probable that it was actually from a fatal mixture of drugs and alcohol. "It was real sad," a close family friend later recalled for an interviewer. "Gladys only wanted to make Elvis proud of her. She just wanted him to be proud. But she kept on taking those pills, and drinking..."

Elvis reached his mother's bedside moments after she died in a Memphis hospital, and he stayed alone with her dead body for only a minute or two. Then he came stoically out, walked down a hall to an empty waiting room, slumped down in a chair, and burst into tears. A couple of days later, after his mother had been buried, Elvis and his father stood together for a time on the front steps at Graceland. "Look, Daddy," sobbed Elvis, pointing to chickens that his mother had kept on the front lawn of the estate, "Mama won't never feed them chickens no more." And on her gravestone Elvis later had these words inscribed: "She was the sunshine of our house."

Arriving in Frankfurt, West Germany, for Army posting

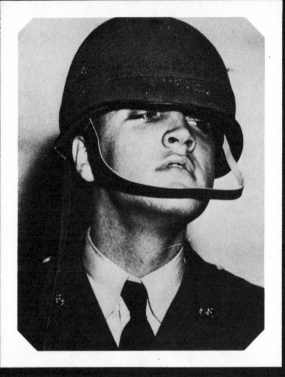

Trying out steel helmet, part of new gear issued at Army base in Friedberg, West Germany, October 3, 1958

Pvt. Elvis Presley

G.I. Elvis with parents

Best Wishes
Elvis Presley

Elvis in uniform

March 5, 1960—Elvis
musters out

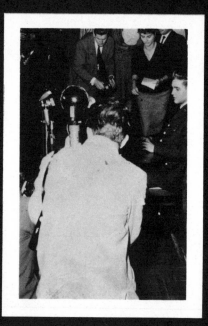

News conference on arrival back
in the U.S., March, 1960

With Margrit Buergin, of Frankfurt, his
"steady date," October 1958

With his father at the Ritters Park Hotel in
Bad Hamburg, West Germany

Nancy Sinatra presenting Elvis with gift from her famous father at Fort Dix, New Jersey, March 3, 1960

In late September of 1958, as the press swarmed around the Military Ocean Terminal in Brooklyn and an Army band played "All Shook Up," Elvis sailed off to Germany on a troop ship. And he spent the rest of his fairly uneventful military career as a scout Jeep driver assigned to an armored unit stationed in Friedberg, Germany, not far from Frankfurt. Said Elvis's top sergeant, "He scrubs, washes, greases, paints, marches, runs, carries his laundry, and worries through inspections just like everyone else." In short, Elvis got no special or favored attention while in the Army, although he lived off base in Friedberg with his widowed father, who'd come to Germany to keep him company.

In early March, 1960, Elvis was flown back from Germany with a planeload of other troops to Fort Dix, New Jersey, where—with a good deal of hoopla that had been arranged by Colonel Parker—he was honorably discharged from the Army with the rank of sergeant. He'd been a good soldier.

With producer Hal B. Wallis, discussing Elvis' first post-Army Hollywood feature

TV Guide *announcement for May 12, 1960,*
Timex show

ack in civilian life, Presley pretty much
picked up his career where he'd dropped
it in 1958. He immediately began making records again, for instance, and he amazingly soon
had yet another string of Number 1 hits and
million-copy sellers, including "It's Now or
Never" and "Are You Lonesome Tonight?" What
was significant about these new hits, however,
was that they weren't rock 'n' roll numbers but
ballads, of the sort that Pat Boone or Perry
Como could just as easily have recorded. The
reason: Colonel Parker had made a command
decision that rock 'n' roll was dead and that
Elvis could only survive by going along with
what the mass public wanted. Which, of course,
was exactly the opposite of the way that he'd got
to the top in the first place. Still, as always, Presley did what the Colonel told him to do.

Shortly after getting out of the Army, Elvis
picked up $125,000 for doing six minutes on a
Frank Sinatra TV special, and he then headed
off to Hollywood to make his first post-Army

Priscilla Beaulieu plays an Elvis record at home in Wiesbaden, West Germany. Miss Beaulieu, daughter of an Air Force captain, was Elvis' steady date in early 1960

movie, entitled, appropriately enough, *G.I. Blues*. The new picture, which was simultaneously released in more than five hundred theaters in October, 1960, turned out to be a service farce with a score of Tin Pan Alley-type songs that sounded as though they might have come from a 1940s' Doris Day musical. "When they took the boy out of the country, they apparently took the country out of the boy," said Jim Powers in the *Hollywood Reporter*. "It is a subdued and changed Elvis Presley who has returned from military service in Germany to star in Hal Wallis's *G.I. Blues*." And, added Powers, "the picture will have to depend on the loyalty of

**With Joey Bishop, Frank Sinatra, and Nancy Sinatra
on Sinatra-Timex TV special**

The puppet sequence
of G.I. Blues

On the set of G.I.
Blues with Shirley
MacLaine

With Juliet Prowse in
G.I. Blues

Babysitter Elvis in
G.I. Blues

With James Douglas,
Mickey Knox, and
Arch Johnson in G.I.
Blues

Madcap publicity
pose for G.I. Blues
with Juliet Prowse

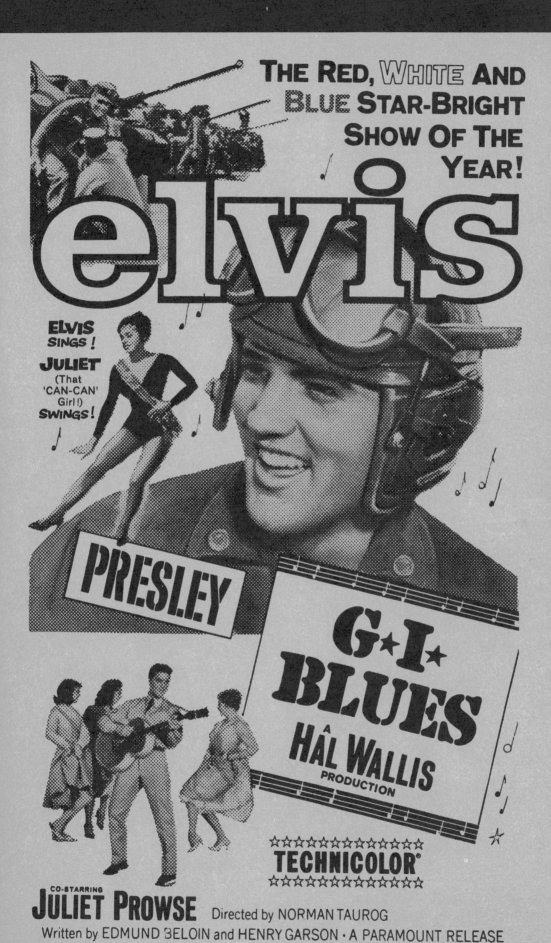

Advertisement for G.I. Blues (1960)

Candid shot taken in 1960

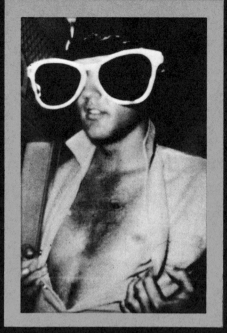

*Teasing the press at news conference
in Beverly Wilshire Hotel, 1960*

**Being inducted into the Los Angeles Indian Tribal Council by Chief Wah-Nee-Ota,
December 1960, in recognition for his "constructive portrayal of a man of
Indian blood" in 20th Century-Fox's Flaming Star**

Back home and swamped, as usual, by his fans

Presley fans to bail it out at the box office." And bail it out they did, for *G.I. Blues* grossed $4.3 million in the United States and Canada alone and was one of 1960's biggest box-office hits. But even his most dedicated fans agreed that a new Elvis had emerged in *G.I. Blues*—the days of the long hair, of the gyrating pelvis, and of "Good Rockin' Tonight" were apparently gone for good. Which was exactly as Colonel Parker wanted things—the image of Presley as the easygoing regular guy who cheerfully did his hitch in the Army was now also to be his image

On the set of Flaming Star *with director Don Siegel*

Advertisement for Flaming Star (1960)

With Rudolph Acosta in Flaming Star

With Dolores Del Rio in Flaming Star

74

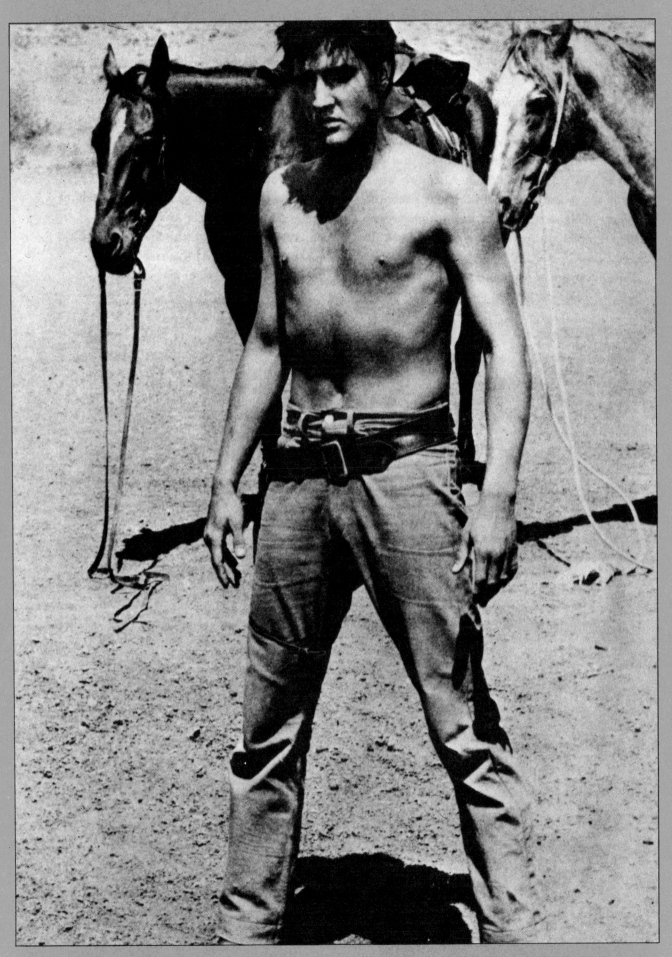

As Pacer in Flaming Star

Growth of the Elvis Presley fan clubs

I am a
loyal Elvis Fan

I collect all of his
records and pictures,
and see all of
his movies

Sharon Fox

ure

— Elvis Presley Fan Club —

THIS IS TO CERTIFY THAT

Miss Sharon Fox

Chicago 30, Illinois

IS AN OFFICIAL MEMBER OF THE

— ELVIS PRESLEY FAN CLUB —

ELAINE PASENSKY, Pres.

Oct. 30, 1959

Elvis Presley Tankers

MEMPHIS, TENNESSEE

This Certifies that

Miss. Sharon Fox

IS A MEMBER IN GOOD STANDING

Oct. 1 1961 (Honorary)

Date

ELVIS PRESLEY, Honorary President
GARY PEPPER, Active President
793 Eva Street — — Memphis, Tenn.

Our Motto! "Tanks' For The Memories"
of Elvis' splendid service record.

Sharon Fox

This Is To Certify That You Are Now
Officially One Of

**ELVIS PRESLEY'S
GOLDEN PLATTERS**

AIM: "We Aim To Keep 'em Golden"
MOTTO: "A Golden Voice —
— A Golden Platter"

ELVIS PRESLEY
Honorary President

Mildred Eaton, President

in the movies and on records. In short, Colonel
Parker was calculatedly turning Elvis into a
kind of latter-day Bing Crosby.

For a long time, the new Elvis seemed to be
just as successful as the old Elvis with his loyal
public, who were themselves now a bit more

With Tuesday Weld in Wild in the Country

With Millie Perkins in Wild in the Country

With Hope Lange in Wild in the Country

On the set of Wild in the Country *with Colonel Parker (center) and director Philip Dunne*

With William Mims, John Ireland, and Hope Lange in Wild in the Country

Dispensing with his guitar for a moment, Elvis swings a mean right——and connects

With Joan Blackman (in water) in Blue Hawaii

On the set of Blue Hawaii (1961) with Barbara Walters (at table, left) and Joan Blackman (right of Presley)

With Joan Blackman, Roland Winters, and Angela Lansbury in Blue Hawaii

Blue Hawaii

With Joan Blackman in Blue Hawaii

With Colonel Parker and Memphis Mayor Henry Loeb, 1961

On location in Seattle for It Happened at the World's Fair, 1962

With friend Johnny Cash in 1961

Belated twenty-seventh-birthday salute for Elvis in Las Vegas from his friend, hotelman Milton Prell

mellow than they'd been in 1956. Throughout the 1960s, Elvis continued to make his movies, lightweight musicals with titles like *Girl Happy, Tickle Me, Paradise—Hawaiian Style;* and *Harum Scarum* in which he was co-starred with the likes of Shelley Fabares, Ann-Margret, Mary Ann Mobley, and Nancy Kovack. And for quite a while the pictures continued to make money. In 1966, for example, Presley earned $5 million, most of which came from his movies.

Still, Elvis's career went into a decline in the 1960s, and from the spring of 1962 until the

The informal Elvis

winter of 1969 he didn't have a single Number 1 record. The problem was that a new generation of teen-agers had come along who were into Bob Dylan, the Beatles, the Rolling Stones, and the hard-rock sound of groups like the Jefferson Airplane. And who looked upon Elvis as a back number, even though many of the most popular singers and groups of the 1960s, including the Beatles, admitted to having been heavily influenced by Elvis. From 1962 to 1969, moreover, Elvis made no public appearances. He divided all of his time between Graceland and various Los Angeles houses that he rented. And he once again took up the life style that he'd led before going into the Army. The nonstop parties—complete with the Memphis Mafia, the girls, and the Pepsi-Cola—were resumed. Once more, too, it was fun-and-games time, complete with a live

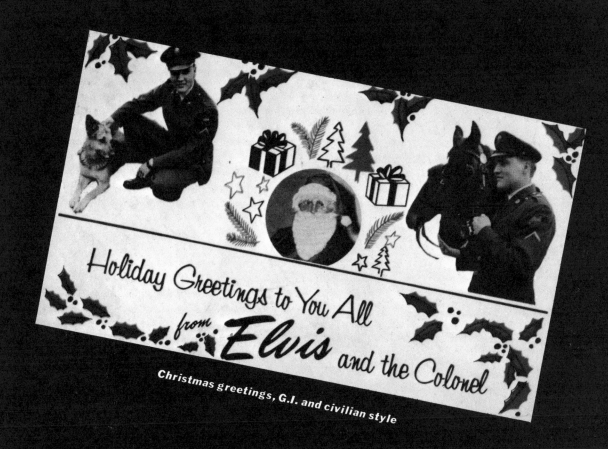

Christmas greetings, G.I. and civilian style

Elvis and the Colonel in Hollywood, 1962

in pet chimpanzee, water-pistol fights, and flame-thrower fights (with butane lighters Elvis and his buddies cut the ends off of).

But if he went in for a good deal of childish horseplay, Elvis still didn't drink, or smoke anything stronger than an occasional small Dutch cigar, and his only vice, aside from a penchant for womanizing, was a serious tendency to overeat. And he ate almost nothing but junk—cheeseburgers, French fries, peanut-butter-and-banana sandwiches, and burnt bacon were

his favorite foods. From such a diet, Elvis began to put on a good deal of weight in the mid 1960s, which then led him to go on a series of crash programs to lose it. But he nonetheless gradually got fatter, to the point where he could no longer stand to look at himself in his movies. He grew sullen, reclusive, and uncharacteristically mean-tempered. He kicked in the fronts of several TV sets, smashed a pool table, broke up an expensive guitar, and on one occasion, when he'd arrived home late to find the

★ ELVISGRAM ★

ELVIS PERFORMS FOR CHARITY
FEBRUARY 25, 1961 — *MEMPHIS*
ELVIS DID SHOW RAISING SUM OF
$52,000 — ALL WENT TO CHARITY
MARCH 25, 1961 — HAWAII
ELVIS' SHOW RAISES $67,000 FOR BENEFIT
OF ARIZONA WAR MEMORIAL

AWARDSVILLE FOR THE KING
APRIL 1961 NATIONAL RECORD MANUFACTURERS
ASSOCIATION GAVE THE FOLLOWING AWARDS
(1) BEST MALE ARTIST OF 1960 — ELVIS PRESLEY
(2) BEST SONG 1960 "NOW OR NEVER" BY ELVIS
(3) BEST SELLING LP 1960 GI BLUES BY ELVIS

1960-1961   ELVIS WINS
17 AWARDS IN TV AND RADIO POLLS
ELVIS SWEEPS AMERICAN BANDSTAND 5TH YR.
WINS 12 AWARDS — MAGAZINES AND PAPER POLLS
FOR 5 TH YEAR
ELVIS WINS ANNUAL EUROPEAN POPULARITY POLL
LOS ANGELES MIRROR ANNUAL MUSIC POLL
TV STAR PARADE POLL

DID YOU KNOW ?
ELVIS HAS 39 GOLD RECORDS
FOR MILLION SELLERS
ELVIS' TOTAL RECORD SALES
TO DATE — 77 MILLION !!

COMPILED BY: HELEN HUBER, CHICAGO, ILL.
PRINTED BY: MILDRED EATON, CHANNELVIEW, TEX.

Keeping the public alerted to Elvis' accomplishments

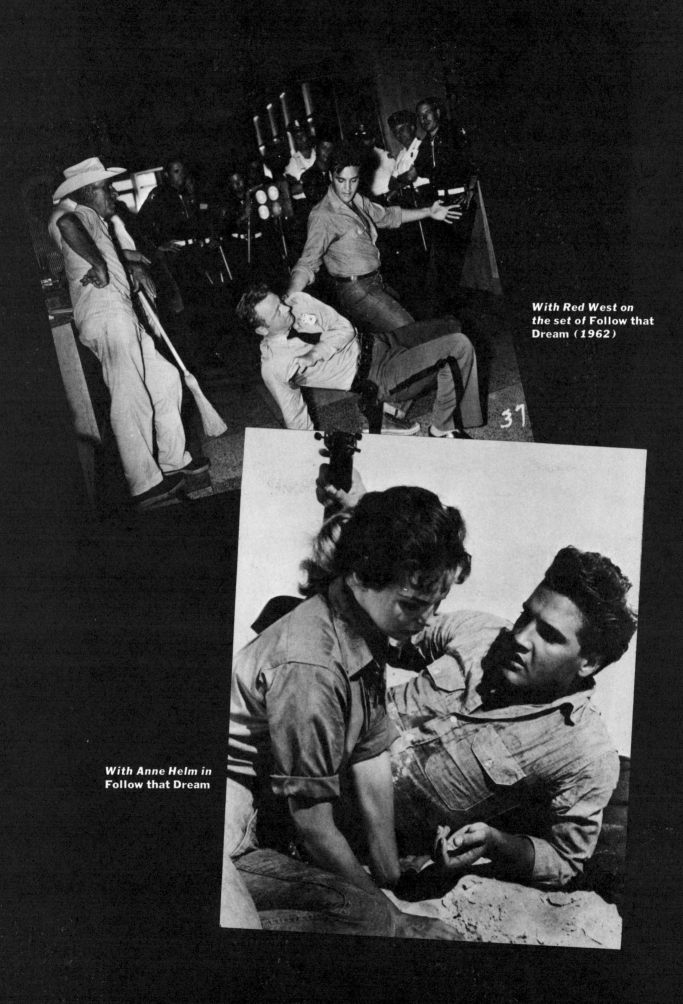

With Red West on the set of Follow that Dream (1962)

With Anne Helm in Follow that Dream

Follow that
Dream

With Anne Helm, Arthur O'Connell, and the "brood" in publicity shot for Follow that Dream

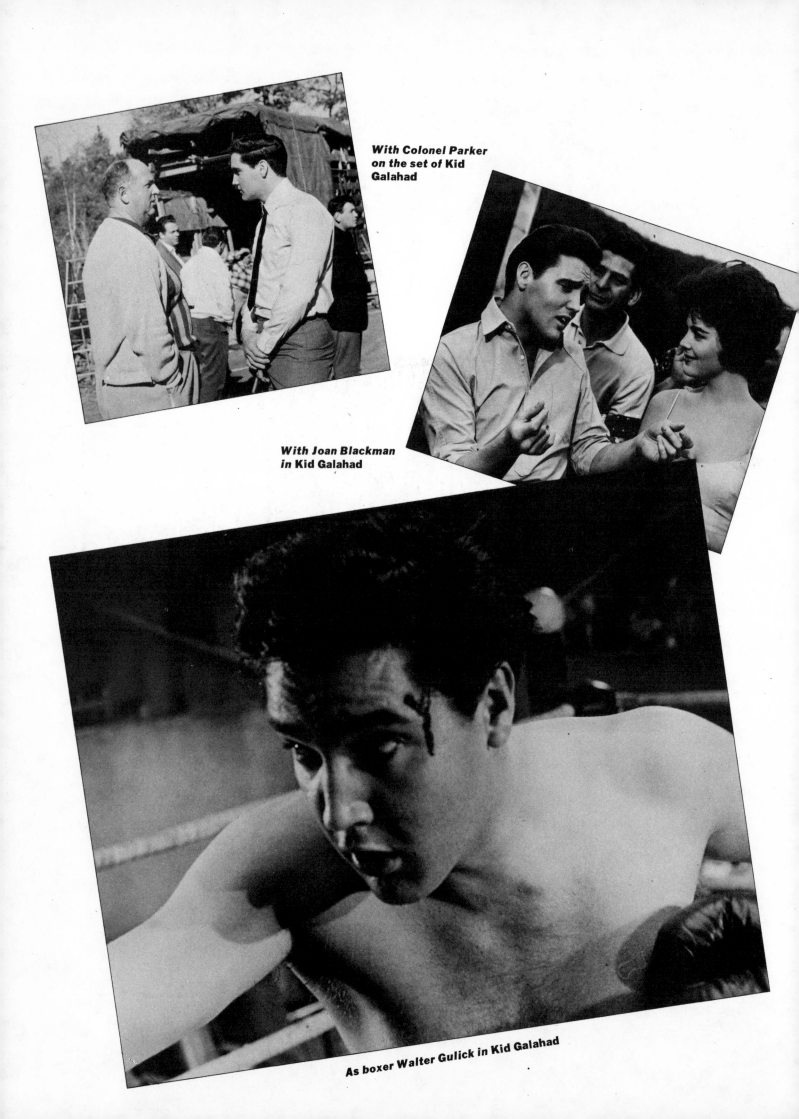

With Colonel Parker on the set of Kid Galahad

With Joan Blackman in Kid Galahad

As boxer Walter Gulick in Kid Galahad

With Joan Blackman and Lola Albright in a publicity pose for Kid Galahad (1962)

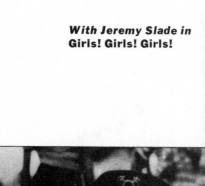

With Jeremy Slade in Girls! Girls! Girls!

On the set of Girls! Girls! Girls!

With Laurel Goodwin in Girls! Girls! Girls! *(1962)*

With Ginny and Elizabeth Tiu, and Laurel Goodwin in Girls! Girls! Girls!

SELL THE KIDS VIA
COLORING CONTEST

Coloring contests always go over big with the younger set. Aim for that market by planting this specially prepared art in the newspaper and/or getting a cooperating store to use it in herald form as package stuffers. Offer guest tickets, records and any other prizes you can promote to the first so-many most attractively colored entries.

(Copy for contest)

HEY, KIDS! COLOR THIS SCENE FROM "GIRLS! GIRLS! GIRLS!" . . . YOU MAY WIN TICKETS TO SEE THE NEW ELVIS PRESLEY MUSICAL . . . PLUS OTHER PRIZES!

See how good an artist you are! Send your completed picture to Contest Editor at this paper no later than . . . .

(date)

Promotional material for Girls! Girls! Girls!

With Yvonne Craig in
It Happened at the
World's Fair

It Happened at the World's Fair

On location in Seattle for It Happened at the World's Fair

With Joan O'Brien in It Happened at the World's Fair (1963)

With Vicky Tiu in It Happened at the World's Fair

95

In Fun in Acapulco

**With Ursula Andress
and Paul Lukas in
Fun in Acapulco**

**With Ursula Andress
and Larry Domasin
in Fun in Acapulco**

In Fun in Acapulco (1963)

FUN IN ACAPULCO

With Glenda Farrell and Arthur O'Connell (right) in Kissin' Cousins

Kissin' Cousins

As Josh Morgan and Jodie Tatum in Kissin' Cousins (1964)

With Yvonne Craig and Pamela Austin in publicity pose for Kissin' Cousins

With Ann-Margret in Viva Las Vegas

With Ann-Margret in Viva Las Vegas

With Nicky Blair, Roy Engel, William Demarest, and Ann-Margret in Viva Las Vegas

Advertisement for
Viva Las Vegas
(1964)

*With Barbara Stan-
wyck in Roustabout*

*With Sue Ane Lang-
don in Roustabout*

With Barbara Stanwyck, Joan Freeman, and Leif Erickson in Roustabout

Advertisement for Roustabout (1964)

With Jimmy Hawkins,
Gary Crosby, and
Joby Baker in Girl
Happy

Singing and dancing
the Crab with Shelley
Fabares, while Jimmy
Hawkins plays guitar
in Girl Happy

With Lynn Edginton,
Chris Noel, Shelley
Fabares, and John
Fiedler in Girl Happy

Advertisement for Girl Happy (1965)

With Shelley Fabares in Girl Happy

**With Jocelyn Lane
and Jack Mullaney in
Tickle Me**

**As Lonnie Beale in
Tickle Me**

In Tickle Me (1965)

TICKLE ME

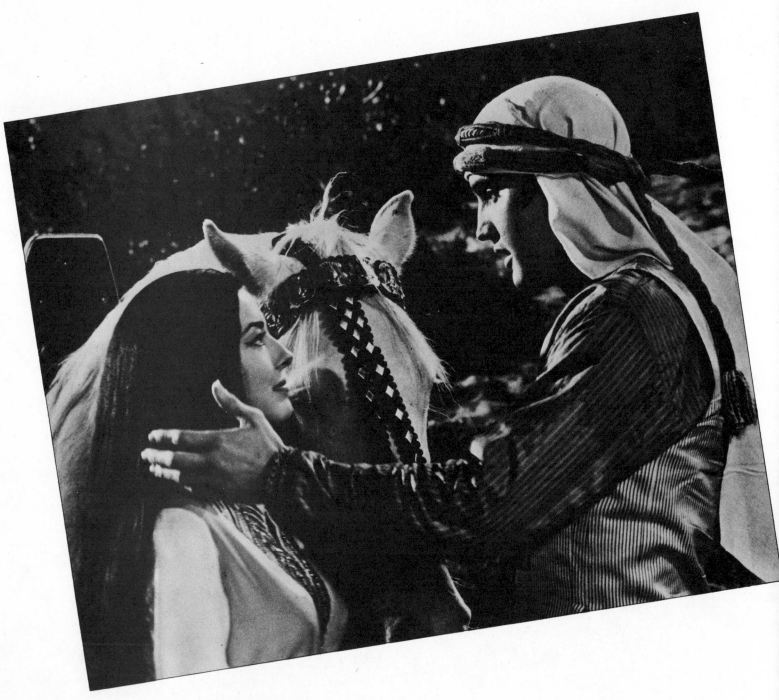

With Carolyn Carter
in Harum Scarum

In **Harum Scarum**

In **Harum Scarum**

As the contemporary Rudolph Valentino in Harum Scarum

As the singing lead of Frankie and Johnny

With Harry Morgan, Donna Douglas, and Nancy Kovack in Frankie and Johnny

With Donna Douglas in Frankie and Johnny

Advertisement for Frankie and Johnny (1966)

With Donna Butterworth in Paradise, Hawaiian Style

In Paradise, Hawaiian Style

SPINOUT

In **Spinout** (1966)

In **Spinout**

*With Carl Betz,
Jimmy Hawkins,
Deborah Walley, and
Jack Mullaney in
Spinout*

*With Shelley
Fabares, Deborah
Walley, and Diane
McBain in Spinout*

Receiving a youth leadership award in 1966

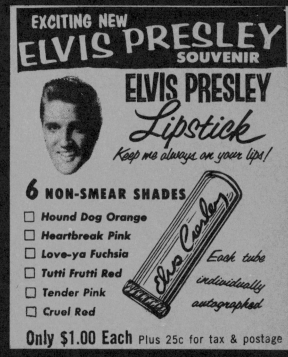

Merchandising . . . .

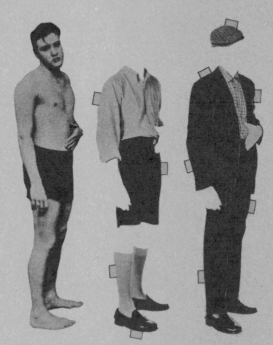

CUT-OUT DOLLS FOR GROWN-UP GIRLS

Urbane Elvis, man of distinction, mingles unnoticed with men of quality and affairs: the perfect choice to save embarrassment among diplomats, cosmopolitans and denizens of any city boulevard.

.... the star

gates of Graceland locked, crashed angrily through the gate at seventy miles an hour in a Rolls-Royce limousine.

Elvis's temper tantrums were perhaps particularly difficult for his friends and family to deal with, because he'd always before been the polite, soft-spoken, and well-behaved "good boy" that his mother had brought him up to be in East Tupelo. (Of course, he'd been in a few well-publicized fist fights, in the early days, usually with some heckler who'd been riding him about his long hair or his pink jackets.) The di-

rectors of Elvis's movies, too, were constantly impressed at how easy he was to work with, his always saying "Yes, sir" to them and doing exactly as he was told to do. And musicians, engineers, and record-company executives who worked with him on recording sessions also invariably found him easy to get along with. And hard-working. But now, in the mid 1960s, as his career slumped, his waistline expanded, and his hair began to turn prematurely gray (he now dyes it black), he became increasingly temperamental and difficult to get along with.

Kissing the bride

For years, Presley's name had been romantically linked (mainly by press agents) with one Hollywood starlet after another, from Ann-Margret to Kim Novak, Rita Moreno, Shelley Fabares, Judy Sprickles, and Suzanna Leigh. But, of course, he never married any of them, if, in fact, he actually ever dated any of them—Elvis has never been seen at a nightclub, in a restaurant, or at any Hollywood party other than his own. So his romantic life was basically a secret from the public.

While in Germany in the Army, however, Elvis had had a much-publicized romance with a fourteen-year-old American girl named Priscilla Beaulieu, who was the daughter of a U.S. Army major stationed in Frankfurt. Unknown to the public, who assumed that his fling with Priscilla had ended when he left Germany, Elvis had invited her back to America to spend Christmas, 1960, with him at Graceland. And he'd then talked her parents into letting Priscilla stay on and live at Graceland. Elvis's father, Vernon,

Elvis and the former Priscilla Beaulieu being married in Las Vegas by Nevada Supreme Court Justice Davis Zenoff, May 1, 1967. The bride's sister, Michelle Beaulieu (right), is maid of honor.

had married again, to a woman he'd met in Germany named Dee Elliott, and so with Vernon and Dee as kind of surrogate parents, Priscilla moved into Graceland, enrolled in Memphis's Immaculate Conception High School, and saw Elvis only when he was back home between pictures. In June, 1963, Priscilla was graduated from high school, but she continued in the next years to live at Graceland while studying modeling and taking courses at a place called the Patricia Stevens Finishing and Career School.

In 1967, most of Elvis's fans assumed that he hadn't seen Priscilla in years. And so it came as a considerable surprise to them when—on May 1, 1967, in Las Vegas—he suddenly married Priscilla. They were married by a judge in a brief and simple ceremony that was followed, in the Aladdin Hotel, by a huge and garish reception staged by Colonel Parker mainly for the benefit of the press. The entire occasion, in fact, at a time when Elvis's career was seriously slipping, had the smell of an elaborate publicity

Examining the wedding ring

"With this ring, I thee wed."

Cutting the wedding cake

The proud parents preparing to leave Baptist Hospital in Memphis with their four-day-old daughter, Lisa Marie, born February 5, 1968

stunt. In any event, Priscilla and Elvis went off to Palm Springs for a four-day honeymoon and nine months later to the day, on February 1, 1968, had a child, a daughter whom they named Lisa Marie.

Priscilla didn't at all get along with the roistering members of the Memphis Mafia, and they lost no love over her, either. But she won—all but two of them were banished from Elvis's entourage. In February, 1967, Elvis, whose newest interest was horseback riding, had bought a 163-acre ranch about five miles south of Graceland (over the Mississippi border, in Walls) that he dubbed the Circle G. Costing him $250,000, the Circle G was a place where he could ride the stable of horses he'd bought, and it was at the Circle G, rather than at Graceland, that he lived with Priscilla and their infant daughter when they went home to Memphis. Meanwhile, he also bought a $400,000 mansion in the elegant Trousdale section of Los Angeles where he and Priscilla lived when they were in California.

By all accounts, including his own, Elvis never really settled down as a husband and father, and apparently most of the time totally ignored Priscilla and his child. Finally, in 1972, Priscilla simply took Lisa and walked out on Elvis. And on October 9, 1973, they were divorced. Amicably, as they say. Anyway, Priscilla got a settlement of $825,000 in cash, plus $6,000 a month for ten years, a 5-per-cent interest in a pair of music-publishing companies that Elvis owns, and $4,000 a month in child support. No wonder—from Priscilla's point of view, at least—the divorce was amicable. Today, Priscilla lives with Lisa in a $200,000 Los Angeles duplex apartment, co-owns a boutique for which she designs clothes, and never has a bad word to say to anyone about Elvis.

Elvis, Priscilla and Lisa, 1971

On the late 1960s, as a wave of nostalgia
for the 1950s began to hit America,
Elvis's singing career had a bit of an upturn.
He did a fairly successful TV special in 1968
and in the winter of 1969 he had his first Number
1 record in seven years, "Suspicious
Minds," which sold more than a million copies.
And it was soon followed by "Don't Cry,
Daddy," a Mac Davis ballad that—although it
rose no higher than Number 6 in the charts—
also sold a million copies. And he had substantial hits around that time, too, with "Kentucky
Rain" and "In the Ghetto."

Meanwhile, however, Elvis's movie career
had gone all to hell—audiences had simply
stopped going to see his pictures. In the middle
of the 1960s, when Elvis had been riding high
in the movies and making a couple of million
from each of them, Colonel Parker had foxily
figured that they could make even more money
from the pictures if they produced them for

With Dodie Marshall
in **Easy Come, Easy Go**

In **Easy Come, Easy Go**

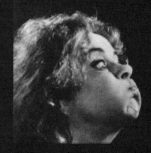

With Elsa Lanchester
in **Easy Come, Easy Go**

With Annette Day in Double Trouble

As singer Guy Lambert in Double Trouble

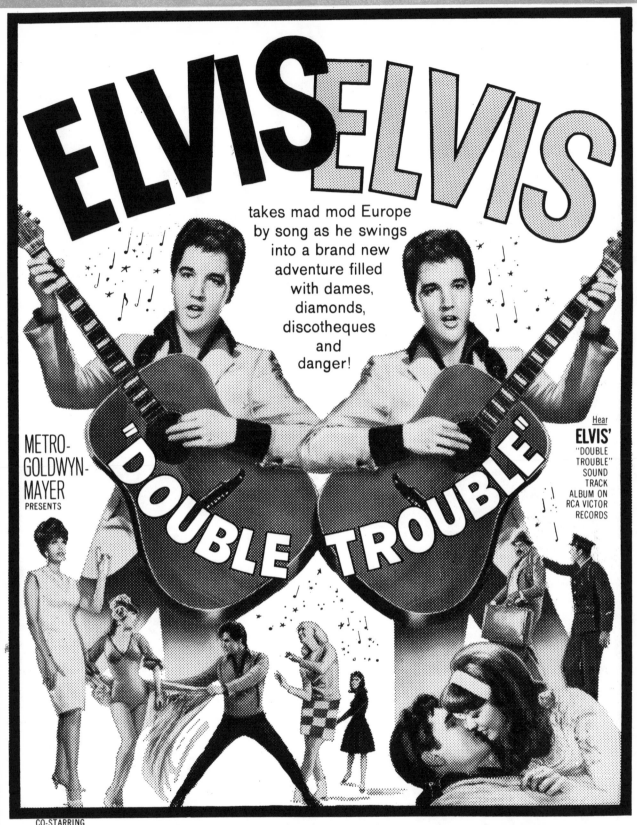

Advertisement for Double Trouble (1967)

With Gary Merrill and Will Hutchins in Clambake

On the set of Clambake with Lee Hazelwood

With Will Hutchins in Clambake

Advertisement for Clambake (1967)

**As Joe Lightcloud in
Stay Away, Joe**

In Stay Away, Joe

**With Joan Blondell
in Stay Away, Joe**

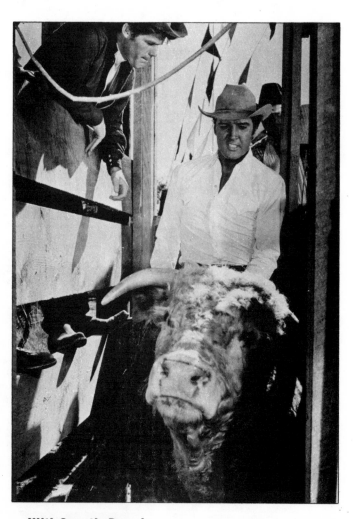

**With Quentin Dean in
Stay Away, Joe**

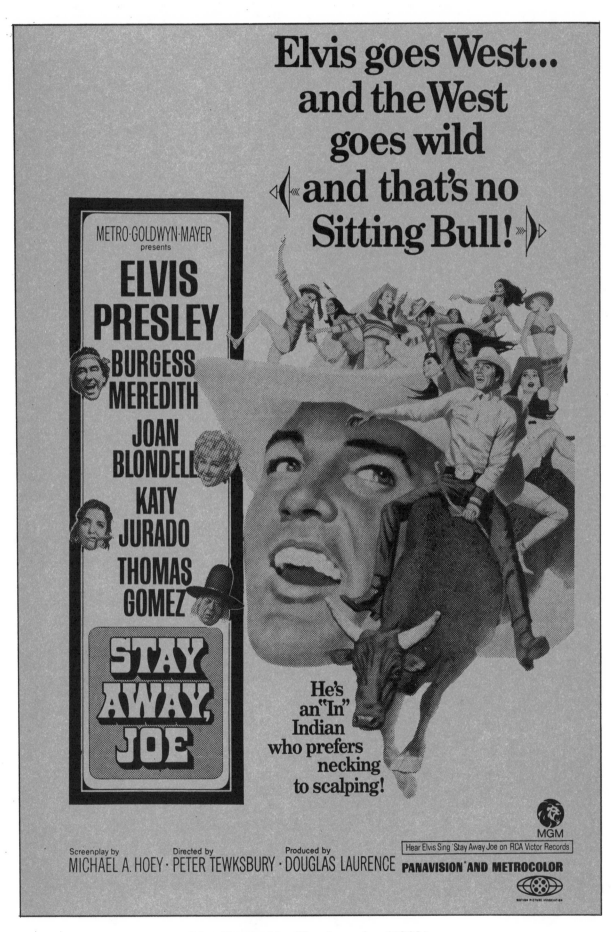

Advertisement for Stay Away, Joe (1968)

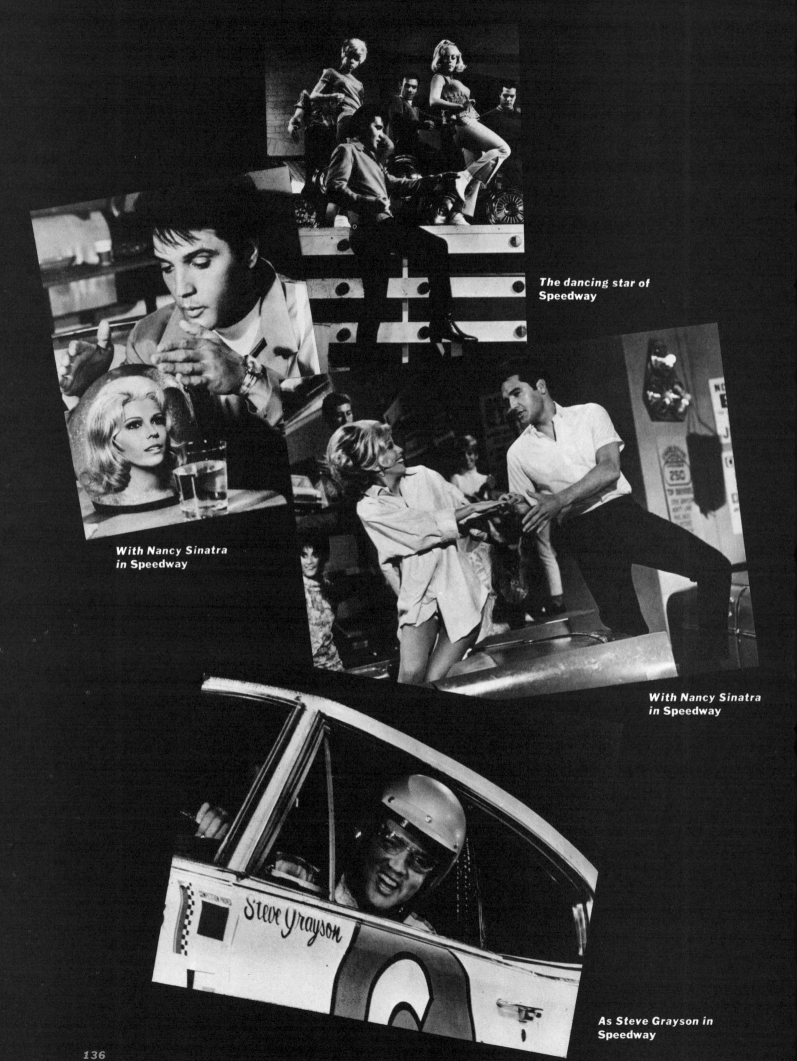

The dancing star of
Speedway

With Nancy Sinatra
in Speedway

With Nancy Sinatra
in Speedway

As Steve Grayson in
Speedway

ELVIS PRESLEY & NANCY SINATRA

smooth, fast and in high gear!

Torrid together... singing... dancing... turning on the romance... as they make the racing scene at the famed furious "Charlotte 600!"

HEAR ELVIS SING his greatest new songs on the RCA VICTOR soundtrack album

METRO-GOLDWYN-MAYER Presents

"SPEEDWAY"

Advertisement for Speedway (1968)

As photographer Greg *in* Live a Little, Love a Little

With Michele Carey in Live a Little, Love a Little

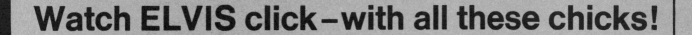

Watch ELVIS click—with all these chicks!

ELVIS shoots the works from dawn to darkroom... as a pin-up photographer who doesn't want to get pinned down!

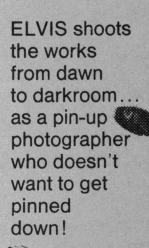

Hear **ELVIS** sing "Almost in Love" and "A Little Less Conversation" on RCA Records.

METRO-GOLDWYN-MAYER
PRESENTS
A DOUGLAS LAURENCE
PRODUCTION
STARRING

ELVIS PRESLEY
shows you how to
LIVE A LITTLE
LOVE A LITTLE

CO STARRING
MICHELE CAREY · DON PORTER · RUDY VALLEE · DICK SARGENT
SCREENPLAY BY
MICHAEL A. HOEY AND **DAN GREENBURG**   BASED ON ... T LIPS" BY DAN GREENBURG
DIRECTED BY   PRODUCED BY
NORMAN TAUROG · DOU...   ...d METROCOLOR   MGM

**Advertisement for
Live a Little, Love a
Little (1968)**

In Live a Little, Love
a Little

139

With Ina Balin in Charro

Promotional for Charro!

140

A DIFFERENT KIND OF ROLE.
A DIFFERENT KIND OF MAN

*On his neck
he wore the
brand of a killer
On his hip he wore
vengeance.*

National General Pictures *presents*

ELVIS PRESLEY
as
CHARRO!

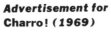

**Advertisement for
Charro! (1969)**

With Sheree North in The Trouble with Girls *(1969)*

THE TROUBLE WITH GIRLS

With director
William Graham on
the set of Change of
Habit

With Mary Tyler
Moore in Change of
Habit

With Barbara McNair
in Change of Habit

144

Caption: **Advertisement for Change of Habit (1969)**

less money. Previously, such Presley films as *Fun in Acapulco* had been budgeted at around $4 million. And so by the Hollywood rule of thumb that a film must gross 2½ times its cost before making a profit, no money was made on a picture like *Fun in Acapulco* until after it had grossed $10 million. And the shooting schedule for a picture like *Fun in Acapulco* or *Viva Las Vegas* was two months or more. But Colonel Parker now made a deal whereby Elvis's pictures would henceforth be produced by "Jungle Sam" Katzman, who was known around Hollywood as the "King of the Quickies." Thus, the first Katzman-produced Presley film, *Kissin' Cousins,* was made on a budget of $1.3 million and shot in seventeen days. The Colonel, who, astonishingly enough, claimed never even to have seen any of Elvis's movies, simply and rather arrogantly figured that Presley's fans would flock to the movies no matter how ineptly they were made. And, after all, a movie that cost $1.3 million to make would begin to show a profit after grossing only $3.25 million. But this time the Colonel may have at last outfoxed himself, because, as Elvis's pictures dropped in quality, the amount of money that they took in began to plummet. To the point where the movies were finally losing money instead of making it. Suddenly, Elvis was box-office poison and washed up in the movies. And now, except for a couple of feature-length documentaries about his doings (*Elvis: That's the Way It Is,* 1970, and *Elvis on Tour,* 1972), he hasn't made a movie since *Change of Habit,* a 1969 bomb in which he played a sensitive but misunderstood singing slum doctor opposite Mary Tyler Moore as the nun he falls in love with.

The collapse of Elvis's movie career was for the most part the fault of the Colonel, who, by the way, can be an extremely unpleasant man. Indeed, the Colonel's personal philosophy can be summed up in his own now-classic line: "You don't have to be nice to the people you meet on the way up if you're not coming back down again."

With Ina Balin in Charro

With his movie career in ruins, and his records selling only moderately well, Elvis turned in 1969 to playing Las Vegas. On July 31, 1969, appearing in public for the first time in seven years, he had a glittering and gala opening at Las Vegas's International Hotel. Billed as the "King of Rock 'n' Roll," he reverted to his raunchy 1956 style, knocking his middle-aged audience dead with driving renditions of "Blue Suede Shoes," "Hound Dog," and others of his earliest hits, sung complete with twitching legs and gyrating pelvis—although the old movements were done now for comic effect. Elvis played the International for a month, at a reported salary of $250,000 per week (only Sinatra and Barbra Streisand earn equal money in Las Vegas), and there wasn't an empty seat in the place during his entire engagement. At least in terms of being an in-person entertainer, Elvis was back on top.

Lovin' 'em tender once again

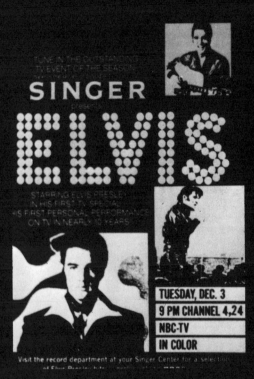

Advertisement for the December 3, 1968, Singer TV special

Elvis in action on the Singer show

Since 1969, Presley has regularly appeared twice a year in Las Vegas, for a month in the summer and another in the winter, at $1 million per engagement, and he's also each year made a national tour, packing them in in such enormous forums as the Houston Astrodome and New York's Madison Square Garden. Nowadays, however, there are few teen-agers in his audiences. Instead, most of those who come to see him are sedate housewives of thirty-five or so —the screaming teen-agers of 1956 grown older, who attend Elvis's concerts perhaps at least partially out of nostalgia for their lost 1950s youth. But, for whatever reason they pay to see him, Elvis remains today one of the most successful entertainers in America, earning around $5 million a year even though he's neither made a movie nor had a hit record in years.

When Priscilla moved out on Elvis, in 1972, the Memphis Mafia immediately moved back in, and Elvis and his buddies once again resumed their fraternity-house life of round-the-clock parties and horseplay. And soon, too, Elvis

There's more than one way to play a guitar!

A thoughtful moment in a busy day

again found himself with a serious weight problem. By the summer of 1974, in fact, he'd bloated up to 240 pounds—when he appeared in Las Vegas, no photographs were allowed to be taken of him, and anyone who tried to had his camera busted by the Memphis Mafia. The Las Vegas audiences were not only appalled at his chubbiness; they also complained that he was no longer giving his all on stage, but was instead mumbling his way through his songs and spending half of his act bickering with some of the onlookers. Explain his friends: "Elvis is exhausted and worn out from too much performing. He used to love it, but now it's an ordeal for him to get through a performance."

On January 8, 1975, Elvis Presley celebrated his fortieth birthday. But it was far from a gala occasion. Instead, on a crash diet that was supposedly designed to get him back down to 180 pounds, he spent the day moping alone in his bedroom at Graceland. A week and a half after that, at 4:00 A.M. on the morning of January 20,

Greetings from Las Vegas

News conference following opening at Las Vegas International Hotel, August 1969

Arriving for the wedding of Delbert B. ("Sonny") West, Jr., his chief security officer, Memphis, December 29, 1970

At Las Vegas International Hotel, August 1970

Performing in Las Vegas, 1969

At the Houston Astrodome, March 1970

In Elvis That's the Way It Is (1970)

Elvis on Tour (1972)

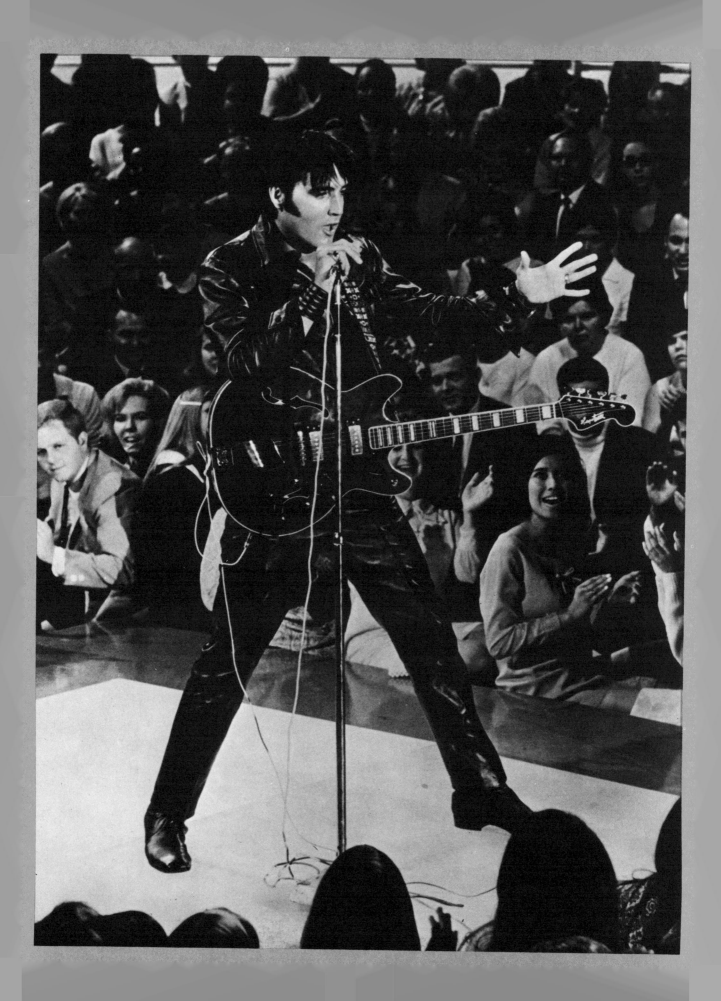

.... I'm all shook up''

With Lamar Fike, Sonny West, Joe Esposito, and the
Colonel at Virginia airport, 1972

Recording session

Two honorees of the U.S. Jaycees Congress of
Ten Outstanding Young Men, Memphis, 1971

At Nassau Coliseum, Long Island, 1973

On the road

Another sellout crowd.

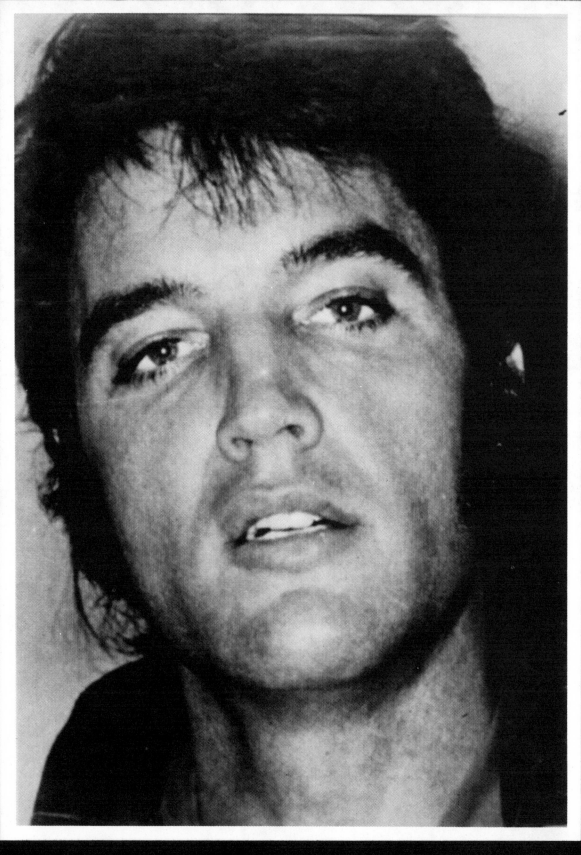

**Elvis, a little tired after another
knock-out performance**

1975, he was rushed to a hospital in Memphis with what was later described as a "blockage of the colon." Once again, he'd been overeating and gaining weight, and the Memphis doctors put him on an all-liquid diet for four weeks. And told him, when he left the hospital, on February 13, to eat more reasonably and to get himself some exercise.

In January, Elvis had displayed interest in buying an airplane. Not that he needed one; he had five already. His collecting habit began, some say, when he noted the publicity that singer John Denver earned "merely" by giving his manager a $40,000 custom Rolls-Royce. Carrying the idea several steps further, Presley presented the Colonel with a full-size, custom-made jet plane worth millions of dollars. But the Colonel—for reasons not made public—refused the offering. Elvis kept the lavish gift for himself.

Already Elvis's personal air fleet rivaled any billionaire's, but the superstar was still not satisfied. Now he surveyed another piece of aerial merchandise—the Boeing 707 jet previously owned by Robert L. Vesco, who had hurriedly left the country while under investigation for a multi-million-dollar stock-manipulation deal. This 707 craft was far different from the commercial airline provided for ordinary passengers. It was more like a flying-type luxury home. The custom-fitted plane was equipped with a dance floor, sauna, gymnasium, office, kitchen, screening room, shower, dressing room, bar, and two bedrooms. The U.S. government had impounded the plane and placed it on the sale market. Elvis made a $75,000 deposit against his $1.5 million purchase offer for it. By September, however, Elvis no longer wanted the jet (he was already selling two of his other planes) and asked for a refund of his down payment. Eventually the 707 was sold at a much lower offer and Presley was sued for the difference.

Another lawsuit sprang from Elvis's fascination with the martial arts. During a demonstration of his karate talent—a private one given for the benefit of some female admirers —one woman was injured, and limped painfully from the room. It turned out that her ankle was broken and Presley was sued for a small fortune in hospital bills. Once again, the singer was asked to make a settlement.

But that was only $10,000 or so, a piddling amount compared to the $6.3 million demanded by a young man who claimed that he was roughly treated by some of Presley's bodyguards when he attempted to crash a private bash hosted by the singer. The victim alleged he was savagely beaten in Presley's presence and that the celebrity not only did nothing to stop the mauling, but actually participated.

Lawsuits are occupational hazards among men so prominently displayed to the worldwide public eye. But to Presley they were signs of persecution. He believed that he had to protect himself from the world-at-large. He became obsessed with security and was rarely seen in public without his corp of bodyguards —the Memphis Mafia. In fact, he was rarely seen at all.

Presley was aware and very proud of his macho image. He became an acknowledged expert at karate and trained himself in the use of all the many weapons in his extensive personal arsenal. He even had himself deputized by the Memphis police force, in September, 1975. His status as a deputy was in keeping with an honorary position in the Federal Drug Enforcement Bureau, assigned to him by President Nixon at Elvis's eager request back in 1971. Members of his own private police force wore uniforms of black pants and white shirts, with a gold badge engraved "Elvis Presley Security." Generally with only these people for company, Elvis spent most of his offstage time on his sprawling Graceland estate in Memphis.

The chief distraction which enlivened this palatial prison was the procession of Presley's girlfriends. For a while he alternated between Linda Thompson, a former Miss Tennessee and a steady Presley companion, and Sheila Ryan. She left him and later married actor James Caan, from whom she is now reportedly separating.

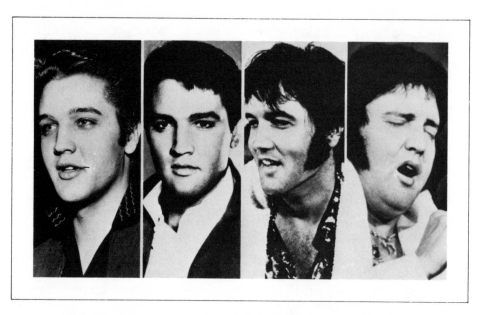

Elvis through the years. From left to right: Elvis in 1957; in the mid-60's; in 1971; in a 1977 performance.

Elvis did not care to have any girlfriend of his be a working lady, so careers were out of the question for them. For their endurance and loyalty they were rewarded primarily with presents—lots and lots of them. Linda, who received the most lavish treatment, acquired hundreds of thousands of dollars in jewelry and clothing, as well as homes for herself (one near Graceland) and her family.

Despite his financial headaches, Presley never lost his generous streak. He performed a benefit concert in May, 1975, which raised $110,000 for victims of the Mississippi tornadoes. A nurse in Memphis Baptist Memorial Hospital, Presley's favorite, was once told to look out the window to see his present to her—a spanking new Grand Prix car. On another occasion he found a woman, a stranger, admiring his Cadillac. He stopped to chat with her and on her next birthday a $11,500 gold-and-white Cadillac was delivered to her home.

Nevertheless, as time wore on, it became more and more improbable that Presley would ever again bump into a stranger. He had always had a reclusive tendency, but now the

forty-year-old singer, concerned as he was about how the visible signs of middle age would affect his public image, became far more publicity-shy. He would retire to his bedroom for weeks at a time. And even when he was with people, they never really knew where his mind was focusing, for he had become increasingly dependent on drugs.

Presley had long relied on drugs, as do many performers who must constantly have the high degree of energy necessary to please their demanding fans. He had used drugs to lull himself to sleep and to zap himself awake in the morning. However, now he employed them to retreat from the world. Apparently he relied mostly on prescription pharmaceuticals, but he consumed them in large doses and in strange combinations. Popping pills may have been responsible for his liver problem, his tremendous fluctuations in weight, and his ongoing battle with glaucoma. (Glaucoma makes the eyes painfully sensitive to light, so during this period he was rarely seen without dark glasses. He had specially tinted contact lenses made for his live performances.)

But his live performances began to dwindle in number, and more of them were canceled for reasons of health. Still, he was recently able to sell out Madison Square Garden for four consecutive shows, something no other single performer had accomplished. *Photoplay* Magazine voted him the top variety star of 1975. And, though Presley's records never again headed the national pop charts the fabulous way they had in the 1950s, they still sold respectably well and would remain in the top 100 for many weeks. In the country-music department his material was still always solid gold. Presley also continued to release about a half-dozen singles a year; these were cut during clandestine sessions of which only a privileged few were aware.

It had already been years since Presley's last movie, but offers continued to flood the Colonel's office. Among those Elvis considered most seriously was a musical of *The World of Suzie Wong,* which would have been a remake of the 1961 film about an American artist and a Chinese prostitute in Hong Kong. *Country Roads,* another possibility, dealt with a jealous country singer who murders his wife. Presley was also offered a reputed $2.5 million to do a stage version of the life of Rudolph Valentino, which was to have been filmed onstage and theatrically released, too.

That Elvis did not undertake these is no great tragedy. However, it would have been intriguing to have seen him opposite Barbra Streisand in *A Star Is Born* (1976). Elvis was her first selection and he was genuinely interested in the movie project. But disagreements about money, and conflicting egos, forced cancelation of the discussions. People soon developed the feeling that no new film projects would ever materialize for Elvis, especially in light of his troublesome weight problems. What's more, without the real star around, onstage or in cinemas, numerous Presley imitators began to appear on the circuit.

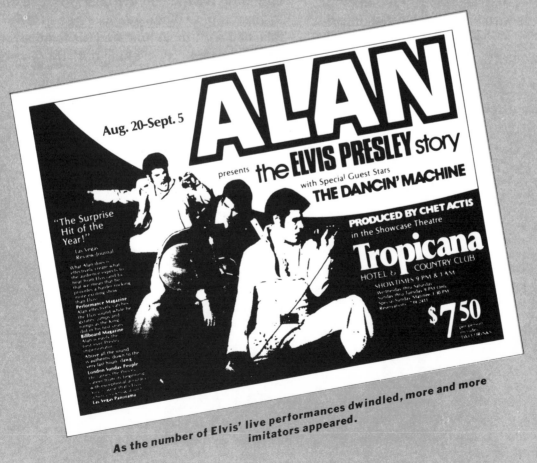

As the number of Elvis' live performances dwindled, more and more imitators appeared.

In the summer of 1976, Presley gave one week's notice to three of his bodyguards: "Red" West, a childhood friend; "Sonny" West, Red's cousin; and Dave Hebler, a karate expert. These three men, especially the Wests, had been with Elvis since his earliest professional days. Their jack-of-all-trades jobs with Elvis were the ones they had held most of their working lives. The sudden dismissal cut the bonds of loyalty to their former employer. Within weeks, they were doing a book with New York *Post* reporter Steve Dunleavy telling the "inside" story of a singer whose public was extremely curious about how he would grow old, or *if* he would grow old.

In August, 1977, Ballantine Books, New York, published the book, a paperback entitled, *Elvis: What Happened?* History provided this publishing event with a tragic counterpoint that led to a surge of renewed public interest in the "King of Rock 'n Roll" and that had resulted in advance orders of over 5 million copies as of this writing.

On Sunday, August 14, 1977, Elvis spent a good deal of time with his nine-year-old daughter, Lisa Marie. (About three weeks prior, he had had his little girl flown to Memphis; on August 8, he had given her a private party at Libertyland amusement park in Memphis, where father and daughter enjoyed the rides together.) That evening he went out shopping for gifts for her, returning to Graceland with a little motorcar which Lisa Marie could drive about the estate. They played with that expensive toy for an hour before she went to bed; Elvis went to sleep at about 6 A.M.

A little after midnight on Monday evening, Presley paid a visit to his dentist. Then, until 4:00 A.M. or so on Tuesday morning, he played racquetball on his own court with twenty-year-old Ginger Alden. She was his latest girlfriend and closely resembled his ex-wife, Priscilla. He and Ginger planned to marry by 1978, she would later insist, and she had an 11½ karat diamond engagement ring to "prove" it.

Thereafter, Elvis retired to his bedroom, where he began reading. About 2:00 P.M. Tuesday afternoon, Elvis's bedside reading light was still burning, but he was not there. At about 2:30 he was found in the bathroom in a curled-up position on the floor, his face buried in the carpet. When he was turned over, his face had a purplish hue, and his tongue (which he had bitten) was sticking out. There were no signs of breathing.

Graceland, Elvis' Memphis home where he died August 16, 1977.

VOL. CXXVI....No. 43,670 © 1977 The New York Times Company   NEW YORK, WEDNESDAY, AUGUST 17, 1977

FINAL

★★★★

DAILY ◉ NEWS

Vol. 59 No. 45   New York, Wednesday, August 17, 1977

Clouds and humid, showers. Low 80s. Sunny tomorrow. Details page 87

Price 20 cents

ELVIS PRESLEY DIES AT 42

Singer Suffers Heart Attack

Elvis Presley as he appeared on a special television program in 1973

ELVIS PRESLEY DIES; ROCK SINGER WAS 42

Heart Failure Cited by Coroner
. . . Followed Scorn

Presley Gave Rock Its Style

He Didn't Invent Form, But Did Bestow Image

By JOHN ROCKWELL

Elvis Presley, one of the pioneers of rock and roll, dies in Memphis.
Stories on page 2, other pictures in the centerfold.

Elvis: Idol of Millions—Se...

TODAY
Showers, low 80s
TONIGHT
Clearing, mild 60s
TOMORROW
Sunny, high 70s
Details page 2
TV: PAGE 50

NEW YORK POST

WEDNESDAY, AUGUST 17, 1977   25 CENTS   Vol. 176. No. 231

© 1977 The New York Post Corporation

METRO
TODAY'S RACING

DAILY PAID
CIRCULATION
2D QUARTER 1977   609,390

The decline is apparent in an older, heavier Elvis Presley as he appeared in a recent concert performance.

MILLIONS MOURN PRESLEY

By LINDSAY MILLER

An entire generation was in mourning today. Elvis Presley, the king of rock 'n' roll, who reshaped American music with the shake of his hips and the beat of his guitar, is dead—at the age of 42.

A preliminary autopsy said an irregular and ineffective heartbeat brought on the heart attack that killed him yesterday afternoon at his Memphis mansion.

A two-hour examination of the body revealed "no evidence of drug abuse," but doctors could not pinpoint the exact cause of Presley's heart problem.

He had been taking drugs—both to fight a persistent hypertension problem and to suppress the appetite which had sent his weight balloon in recent months.

In Memphis, flags were flying at half-staff. It was there that Presley had stayed a recluse for almost 20 years and to which he had given millions in charity.

Presley's divorced wife, Priscilla Beaulieu, and Col. Tom Parker, the promoter who pushed and guided Presley to fame, were flying to Memphis today for tomorrow's funeral.

The services will take place at Graceland, the huge pink colonnaded mansion where Presley was found lying unconscious on a *Continued on Page 8*

EXCLUSIVE New book tells of his decline in a drug nightmare

...that of the ex-partner...
...Presley during his last years is shockingly portrayed in the new book "Elvis: What Happened?"

It was written by Post reporter Steve Dunleavy with the men who were closest to Elvis, his bodyguards Delbert and Red West and Dave Hebler.

A digest of the book, which was to have begun running in The Post next week, has been moved up to start today—

...die as a result of the great entertainer's tragic death.

Among its startling revelations:
- Elvis' drug habit was so bad toward the end that he had to take pills to perform, to sleep, to get up—even to go to the bathroom.
- He was fascinated with guns and once bought 32 pistols in one month. He would sometimes shoot out the screen of a TV set if it showed a program he didn't like.
- At the same time, Presley lived...

...in terrible fear of being assassinated. He instructed the bodyguards to "rip the eyeballs out" of anyone who killed him before the assailant could be brought to trial.
- He ordered the bodyguards to kill the man who had taken his wife...

...from him. And on one occasion he told Elvis to being a drug pusher for him to ease the himself.
- He believed that he had a Christ-like supernatural power, had been put on earth to help people and possessed psychic healing abilities.

Start reading it today— 4-page pullout begins on P. 33

Elvis' death made headlines throughout the world.

The first help to appear was his bodyguard Al Strada; Joe Esposito arrived soon after. He put his ear to the singer's heart and said to the others, "I can't hear anything." When Dr. Nichopoulos reached the scene, he summoned an ambulance. Meanwhile, Elvis's father, and a nurse who was staying on the premises, had reached the bathroom and managed to pry open Presley's mouth to avoid further damage to his tongue. Lisa Marie, drawn to the suite by the noise and confusion, was shunted to another room.

Presley's pulseless, unconscious body was driven seven miles by ambulance to Baptist Memorial Hospital. During the trip, Nichopoulos implored constantly, "Come on breathe, breathe for me." At home, the singer's family and friends were praying for a miracle. At the hospital, an hour later, Elvis was pronounced dead.

It was Dr. Nichopoulos who returned to Graceland with the news, telling Vernon Presley that his son was indeed dead. In turn, Vernon told Lisa Marie of her daddy's death. Reputedly, it was the nine-year-old who phoned the news of the tragedy to the West Coast. Meanwhile, at Graceland, Vernon Presley reportedly broke down in tears, saying, "What am I going to do? Everything is gone!"

Within minutes, as the news of Presley's death spread outward, a crowd of hundreds began to accumulate at Graceland. The Memphis telephones were jammed with calls. It was the first sign of a hysteria that was to overwhelm America and spread throughout the world. In its snowballing impact, it outdistanced the reaction to the deaths of Rudolph Valentino, James Dean, Marilyn Monroe, and Judy Garland. In Memphis the flag was lowered to half-mast and radio stations across the country proceeded to pay tribute to Elvis in the best possible way—by his music.

Elvis' fans mourn him as they crowd around the gates at Graceland the morning after his death was announced.

*Mourners view the crypt before Elvis' entombment
there on August 18, 1977.*

A three-hour autopsy, headed by Dr. Jerry Francisco, the county medical examiner, concluded that heart stoppage was the major cause of death. According to the reports, the singer's heart was enlarged by over one-third its normal size.

The next day, Presley fans from all over the nation began to line up at Graceland for an opportunity to view the body of their idol. Special flights to Memphis brought in the faithful, and some forty National Guardsmen kept them in line. Approximately 100,000 followers arrived, of whom about 75,000 were permitted to view the body (54 at a time). The late singer was dressed in a cream-colored suit, a light blue shirt, and silver tie—with diamond stickpin and cuff links. Vanloads of flowers arrived in Memphis for the following day's funeral.

A lot of loyal pilgrims were unable to bid a final farewell to their king and went home disappointed. For others the day was even worse. Many fainted in the sweltering heat; one man had a heart attack; and a pregnant lady had to be rushed to the hospital. Two of the congregated were killed, and one injured, when a car crossed a road divider and plowed into the viewing line.

In the meantime, millions of orders for Presley discs were being placed, current stocks having been quickly exhausted. Ticketholders for scheduled, sold-out-ahead-of-time Presley concerts were holding on to their expensive tickets en masse, apparently as costly mementoes of their departed hero.

Wednesday evening, a private one-hour service was held at Graceland for Presley. Ex-wife Priscilla, Lisa Marie, Vernon Presley, and his wife, Sheila, were there. Jackie Onassis was reported to have attended. There were fifty family members in all, and 150 guests.

A long line of sixteen white Cadillacs, one a hearse carrying Elvis' body, moves down Elvis Presley Boulevard in Memphis toward nearby Forest Hills Cemetery.

The funeral, held on Thursday, August 18, was as Elvis had requested—white. Sixteen white Cadillacs and one white hound dog were in the fifty-car procession. The casket was of bronze, covered with hundreds of red rosebuds. Other decorations included big black-and-pink flower "guitars." The formation traveled four miles down Elvis Presley Boulevard to Forest Hills Cemetery, where his mother had been buried modestly years before. At one point, a grieving girl from the crowd-lined street had to be pulled away from the hearse.

Among the attending at the cemetery were Tennessee governor Ray Blanton, Burt Reynolds, singer James Brown, Sammy Davis, Jr., Ann-Margret (one of Elvis's closest friends from his movie-making days), guitarist Chet Atkins, actor George Hamilton, and Caroline Kennedy (whose coverage of the event was published in *Rolling Stone*). At Vernon Presley's request, the dismissed bodyguards were absent. Banks of flowers had been sent by such notables as Frank Sinatra, Glen Campbell, George Wallace, and O. J. Simpson. The honorary pallbearers were Joe Esposito, Dr. Nichopoulos, Charlie Hodge (Elvis's lead guitarist), Felton Jarvis (his record producer), Lamar Fike (another associate), and Billy Smith (a cousin). The eulogy was delivered by Reverend Rex Humbard. Elvis's coffin was placed in a marble mausoleum decked with over a thousand floral displays.

There were some bizarre reactions to the star's passing. On August 29, four men were suspected by the Memphis police to be involved in a plot to steal Presley's body and hold it for ransom. Forest Hills Cemetery was placed under surveillance and, when three of the group entered the cemetery via a back

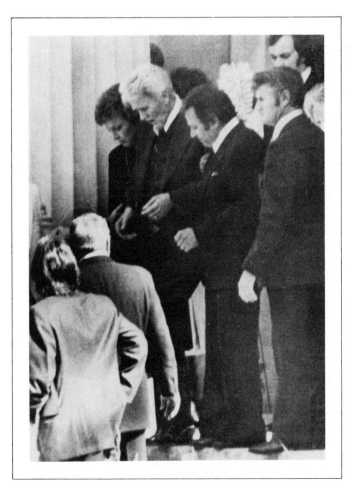

Pallbearers carry the casket
past the thousands of flowers
that covered the area in front
of the mausoleum.

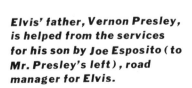

Elvis' father, Vernon Presley,
is helped from the services
for his son by Joe Esposito (to
Mr. Presley's left), road
manager for Elvis.

wall, the law enforcers began to move in. However, the trio became suspicious and started to leave. They were arrested and later arraigned. And then there was the industrious individual who managed to snap photos of the deceased star in his coffin and sold them to a national newspaper for a $75,000 fee.

At this writing, the Presley family is petitioning for an ordinance variance in Memphis so that Elvis and his mother can be reburied on the grounds of Graceland, because the floods of visitors to the Presley plot are ruining the surrounding graves at Forest Hills.

While the funeral was underway in Tennessee, around the world special memorial tributes were made to the late star. A special service sponsored by Elvis's huge British fan club at Christ Church in North London drew such a large crowd that a second service had to be scheduled.

On Tuesday, August 23, Elvis's will was pro-bated in Memphis. His father was named executor. Neither Ginger Alden, one of three people who had witnessed the signing of the will on March 3, 1977, nor ex-wife Priscilla was included in the bequests. The estate totaled nearly $1 million in Memphis real estate; cars, planes, and other tangibles added up to approximately another million dollars. But the biggest asset would be the future royalties for his million-record-selling recordings, enhanced by the additional millions that would be made from reissues of his albums—as well as from older recordings that had never been officially released but soon would be. And then, of course, there would be the merchandising of the Presley memorabilia.

According to the will, Vernon Presley was bequeathed all of Elvis's personal property, "...including trophies and other items accumulated by me during my professional career." Elvis's father will also have "...com-

The crowd at the second memorial service for Elvis at Christ Church, North London. A second service had to be scheduled because so many had to be turned away from the jammed earlier service.

The Forest Hills Cemetery plot in Memphis where Elvis' mother is buried.
The family hopes to rebury both Elvis and his mother on the grounds at Graceland.

plete freedom and discretion as to disposal of any and all such property so long as he shall act in good faith and in the best interest of my estate." The sixty-two-year-old Vernon Presley is to distribute the net income from the estate for the benefit of himself, the late star's daughter, Lisa Marie, and Elvis's eighty-five-year-old grandmother, Minnie Mae. Upon Vernon's and Minnie Mae's demise, all remaining assets of the trust will transfer to Lisa Marie, when she reaches the age of twenty-five. Another provision of the document allows Vernon to provide for "...such other relatives of mine living at the time of my death who in the absolute discretion of [Vernon Presley]...are in need of emergency assistance." Probate Judge Joseph W. Evans estimated the will to be "...the biggest ever filed in the state of Tennessee."

The occasion of Elvis's death led to the compilation of some staggering statistics regarding his phenomenal more-than-two-decade career.

By 1977, more than 600 million singles and albums had been sold internationally; 100 million since 1975. Of his fifty-five million-record-selling singles, "Hound Dog" and "Don't Be Cruel" each sold more than 8 million copies. "It's Now or Never" was reported to have over 1.25 million sales within a three-week period of its mid-1960 distribution. Of his LP albums, twenty-four were certified gold sellers. The *Blue Hawaii* soundtrack sold 5 million records. His thirty-three films grossed over $1.5 million. Since 1969, when he resumed public appearances (in the U.S. only, and with no outdoor dates), he performed in about fifty one-night engagements per year. On these short tours, the average evening gross was $100,000. It has been estimated that the overall gross of Presley's diversified entertainment activities exceeded $4.3 billion.

In the wake of the shock that followed Presley's sudden death, there was time to assess and appreciate the various tributes paid to him. *Photoplay* Magazine readers had recently named Presley their "Favorite Star" and "Favorite Rock Music Star." There were plans to enter Presley in the Rock Hall of Fame. In its evaluation of Presley, the New York Times referred to him as "...the first and greatest American rock-and-roll star ...whose throaty baritone and blatant sexuality redefined popular music." In summation, the *Times* stated, "Elvis will remain the founder of rock-and-roll in most people's minds, and every rock singer owes something to him in matters of inflection and visual style...Elvis was and remained a working-class hero, a man who arose from obscurity and transformed American popular art in answer to his own needs."

Among those persons offering tribute to the late star were:

Frank Sinatra: "There have been many accolades uttered about his talent and performances through the years; all of which I agree with wholeheartedly. I shall miss him dearly as a friend. He was a warm, considerate and generous man."

Ann-Margret: "I've lost a very dear friend. And the world has lost a great entertainer. Not only was Elvis a legend in his own time, but his unique talents will be more appreciated in the years to come."

Paul Simon: "Well, we're definitely grown-ups now. If he's dead, then we can't be kids anymore. It's a very unpleasant and unhappy time for me. The effect of his lifetime is well marked. The effects of his death are startling, yet just beginning to take hold."

In the United States, several TV companies hastily prepared documentaries of the legend, while in both America and abroad the rush is on to film the life story of the "King of Rock 'n' Roll." Special LP packages of Presley's songs are expected to be a big item in the years to come, as are assorted as-told-to and I-remember-Elvis books.

The Reverend Rex Humbard, the TV evangelist, who was the primary speaker at Presley's funeral, related that in December, 1976, he was beckoned to a Las Vegas hotel. The way Humbard recollects it, the distraught singer was teary, and said, "Christ is gonna come real soon...isn't he?" Humbard and the rock star then talked for a half-hour, mostly about the Scriptures. Says Humbard now, "I think it was a premonition or something. He was reaching for something spiritual and I think he found some of what he was looking for."

In the final analysis, not even Elvis knew how to explain his success. "I don't know what it is—I just fell into it, really," Presley told an interviewer a while back. "I remember my daddy and me talkin' about it years ago. Laughin'. He looked at me and said, 'What happened, El? The last thing I remember is I was workin' in a paint factory and you was drivin' a truck.' And I remember how, after something big happened along about 1957, I was sittin' at home and found my mama staring at me. I asked her why and she just shook her head and said, 'I don't believe it. I just don't believe it.' And I guess I feel that same way about it still. It just...caught me up."

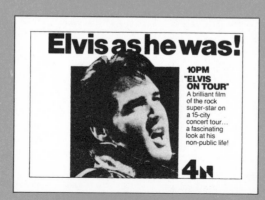

Throughout the world the media paid tribute to Elvis in the weeks following his death.

Elvis Presley Discography

Singles

SUN RECORDS

August 1954   *That's All Right (Mama)/Blue Moon of Kentucky*
SUN 209

October 1954   *Good Rockin' Tonight/I Don't Care if the Sun Don't Shine*
SUN 210

January 1955   *Milkcow Blues Boogie/You're a Heartbreaker*
SUN 215

May 1955   *I'm Left, You're Right, She's Gone/Baby, Let's Play House*
SUN 217

August 1955   *Mystery Train/I Forgot to Remember to Forget*
SUN 223

RCA VICTOR

November 1955   *Mystery Train/I Forgot to Remember to Forget*
RCA 6357

November 1955   *That's All Right (Mama)/Blue Moon of Kentucky*
RCA 6380

November 1955   *Good Rockin' Tonight/I Don't Care if the Sun Don't Shine*
RCA 6381

November 1955   *Milkcow Blues Boogie/You're a Heartbreaker*
RCA 6382

November 1955   *I'm Left, You're Right, She's Gone/Baby Let's Play House*
RCA 6383

January 1956   *Heartbreak Hotel/I Was the One*
RCA 6420

May 1956   *I Want You, I Need You, I Love You/My Baby Left Me*
RCA 6540

July 1956   *Hound Dog/Don't Be Cruel*
RCA 6604

September 1956   *Blue Suede Shoes/Tutti Frutti*
                                RCA 6636

September 1956   *I'm Counting on You/I Got a Woman*
                                RCA 6637

September 1956   *I'll Never Let You Go/I'm Gonna Sit Right Down and Cry Over You*
                                RCA 6638

September 1956   *Tryin' to Get to You/I Love You Because*
                                RCA 6639

September 1956   *Blue Moon/Just Because*
                                RCA 6640

September 1956   *Money Honey/One-Sided Love Affair*
                                RCA 6641

September 1956   *Shake, Rattle and Roll/Lawdy, Miss Clawdy*
                                RCA 6642

September 1956   *Love Me Tender/Any Way You Want Me*
                                RCA 6643

January 1957   *Too Much/Playing for Keeps*
                                RCA 6800

March 1957   *All Shook Up/That's When Your Heartaches Begin*
                                RCA 6870

June 1957   *Teddy Bear/Loving You*
                                RCA 7000

September 1957   *Jailhouse Rock/Treat Me Nice*
                                RCA 7035

December 1957   *Don't/I Beg of You*
                                RCA 7150

April 1958   *Wear My Ring Around Your Neck/Doncha' Think It's Time*
                                RCA 7240

June 1958   *Hard Headed Woman/Don't Ask Me Why*
                                RCA 7280

October 1958   *I Got Stung/One Night*
                                RCA 7410

March 1959   *A Fool Such As I/I Need Your Love Tonight*
                                RCA 7506

June 1959   *A Big Hunk o' Love/My Wish Came True*
                                RCA 7600

March 1960   *Stuck on You/Fame and Fortune*
                                RCA 7740

July 1960   *It's Now or Never/A Mess of Blues*
              RCA 7777

November 1960   *Are You Lonesome Tonight/I Gotta Know*
                  RCA 7810

February 1961   *Surrender/Lonely Man*
                  RCA 7850

May 1961   *I Feel So Bad/Wild in the Country*
             RCA 7880

August 1961   *Little Sister/His Latest Flame*
                RCA 7908

November 1961   *Can't Help Falling in Love/Rock-a-Hula Baby*
                  RCA 7968

February 1962   *Good Luck Charm/Anything That's Part of You*
                  RCA 7992

July 1962   *She's Not You/Just Tell Her Jim Said Hello*
              RCA 8041

October 1962   *Return to Sender/Where Do You Come From*
                 RCA 8100

January 1963   *One Broken Heart for Sale/They Remind Me Too Much of You*
                 RCA 8134

June 1963   *(You're the) Devil in Disguise/Please Don't Drag That String Around*
              RCA 8188

October 1963   *Bossa Nova Baby/Witcher*
                 RCA 8243

October 1963   *Kissin' Cousins/It Hurts Me*
                 RCA 8307

April 1964   *Kiss Me Quick/Suspicion*
               RCA 0639

April 1964   *Viva Las Vegas/What'd I Say*
               RCA 8360

July 1964   *Such a Night/Never Ending*
              RCA 8400

September 1964   *Ain't that Loving You, Baby/Ask Me*
                   RCA 8440

November 1964   *Blue Christmas/Wooden Heart*
                  RCA 0720

March 1965   *Do the Clam/You'll Be Gone*
               RCA 8500

April 1965   *Crying in the Chapel/I Believe in the Man in the Sky*
                                                          RCA 0643

May 1965   *(Such an) Easy Question/It Feels So Right*
                                                          RCA 8585

August 1965   *I'm Yours/(It's a) Long Lonely Highway*
                                                          RCA 8657

October 1965   *Puppet on a String/Wooden Heart*
                                                          RCA 0650

November 1965   *Blue Christmas/Santa Claus Is Back in Town*
                                                          RCA 0647

January 1966   *Tell Me Why/Blue River*
                                                          RCA 8740

February 1966   *Joshua Fit the Battle/Known Only to Him*
                                                          RCA 0651

February 1966   *Milky White Way/Swing Down Sweet Chariot*
                                                          RCA 0652

March 1966   *Frankie and Johnny/Please Don't Stop Loving Me*
                                                          RCA 8780

June 1966   *Love Letters/Come What May*
                                                          RCA 8870

October 1966   *Spinout/All that I Am*
                                                          RCA 8941

November 1966   *If Every Day Was Like Christmas/How Would You Like To Be*
                                                          RCA 8950

January 1967   *Indescribably Blue/Fools Fall in Love*
                                                          RCA 9056

May 1967   *Long Legged Girl (with the Short Dress On)/That's Someone You Never Forget*
                                                          RCA 9115

August 1967   *There's Always Me/Judy*
                                                          RCA 9287

September 1967   *Big Boss Man/You Don't Know Me*
                                                          RCA 9341

January 1968   *Guitar Man/High Heel Sneakers*
                                                          RCA 9425

March 1968   *U.S. Male/Stay Away, Joe*
                                                          RCA 9465

April 1968   *You'll Never Walk Alone/We Call on Him*
                                                          RCA 9600

| May 1968 | Let Yourself Go/Your Time Hasn't Come Yet, Baby |
| | RCA 9547 |

September 1968   A Little Less Conversation/Almost in Love
RCA 9610

October 1968   If I Can Dream/Edge of Reality
RCA 9670

March 1969   Memories/Charro
RCA 9731

April 1969   How Great Thou Art/His Hand in Mine
RCA 0130

April 1969   In the Ghetto/Any Day Now
RCA 9741

June 1969   Clean Up Your Own Back Yard/The Fair Is Moving On
RCA 9747

August 1969   Suspicious Minds/You'll Think of Me
RCA 9764

November 1969   Don't Cry, Daddy/Rubberneckin'
RCA 9768

January 1970   Kentucky Rain/My Little Friend
RCA 9791

May 1970   The Wonder of You/Mama Liked the Roses
RCA 9835

July 1970   I've Lost You/The Next Step Is Love
RCA 9873

October 1970   You Don't Have to Say You Love Me/Patch It up
RCA 9916

December 1970   Rags to Riches/Where Did They Go Lord
RCA 9980

March 1971   I Really Don't Want to Know/There Goes My Everything
RCA 9960

May 1971   Life/Only Believe
RCA 9985

August 1971   I'm Leavin'/Heart of Rome
RCA 9998

October 1971   It's Only Love/The Sound of Your Cry
RCA 1017

November 1971   Merry Christmas Baby/O Come All Ye Faithful
RCA 0572

January 1972   *Until It's Time for You to Go/We Can Make the Morning*
                                                                      RCA 0619

March 1972   *He Touched Me/Bosom of Abraham*
                                          RCA 0651

April 1972   *An American Trilogy/The First Time Ever I Saw Your Face*
                                                                   RCA 0672

September 1972   *Burning Love/It's a Matter of Time*
                                          RCA 0769

November 1972   *Separate Ways/Always on My Mind*
                                          RCA 0815

February 1973   *Fool/Steamroller Blues*
                                  RCA 0910

September 1973   *Raised on Rock/For Ol' Times Sake*
                                          RCA 0088

February 1974   *Take Good Care of Her/I've Got a Thing about You Baby*
                                                             RCA 0196

June 1974   *Help Me/If You Talk in Your Sleep*
                                     RCA 0280

October 1974   *It's Midnight/Promised Land*
                                    RCA 10074

February 1975   *My Boy/Thinking about You*
                                  RCA 10191

March 1976   *Hurt/For the Heart*
                                 RCA 10601

December 1976   *Moody Blue/She Thinks I Still Care*
                                          RCA 10857

June 1977   *Way Down/Pledging My Love*
                                RCA 10998

45 rpm Extended Play (EP) Albums

R.C.A.
1956   Elvis Presley, Vol. 1
          Blue Suede Shoes, I'm Counting on You, I Got a Woman, One-Sided Love Affair
                                                                    RCA EPA 747

1956   Elvis Presley, Vol. 2
          Tutti Frutti, Tryin' to Get to You, I'm Gonna Sit Right Down and Cry,
          I'll Never Let You Go   RCA EPA 1254

1956   Heartbreak Hotel
          Heartbreak Hotel, I Was the One, I Forgot to Remember to Forget, Money Honey
                                                                    RCA EPA 821

1956	Elvis Presley
	Shake, Rattle and Roll, I Love You Because, Blue Moon, Lawdy, Miss Clawdy
	RCA EPA 830

1956	The Real Elvis
	Don't Be Cruel, I Want You, I Need You, I Love You, Hound Dog, My Baby Left Me
	RCA EPA 940

1956 Any Way You Want Me
*Any Way You Want Me, I'm Left, You're Right, She's Gone, I Don't Care if the
Sun Don't Shine, Mystery Train*   RCA EPA 965

1956 Love Me Tender
Love Me Tender, Let Me Be, Poor Boy, We're Gonna Move   RCA EPA 4006

1956 Elvis, Vol. 1
Rip It Up, Love Me, When My Blue Moon Turns to Gold Again, Paralyzed
RCA EPA 992

1956 Elvis, Vol. 2
So Glad You're Mine, Old Shep, Ready Teddy, Anyplace Is Paradise   RCA EPA 993

1957 Strictly Elvis
*Long Tall Sally, First in Line, How Do You Think I Feel,
How's the World Treating You*   RCA EPA 994

1957 Loving You, Vol. 1
Loving You, Party, Teddy Bear, True Love   RCA EPA 1-1515

1957 Loving You, Vol. 2
Lonesome Cowboy, Hot Dog, Mean Woman Blues, Got a Lot o' Livin' to Do
RCA EPA 2-1515

1957 Just for You
*I Need You So, Have I Told You Lately That I Love You, Blueberry Hill,
Is It So Strange*   RCA EPA 4041

1957 Peace in the Valley
Peace in the Valley, It Is No Secret, I Believe, Take My Hand, Precious Lord
RCA EPA 4054

1957 Elvis Sings Christmas Songs
*Santa Bring My Baby Back, Blue Christmas, Santa Claus Is Back In Town,
I'll Be Home for Christmas*   RCA EPA 4108

1957 Jailhouse Rock
*Jailhouse Rock, Young and Beautiful, I Want to Be Free, Don't Leave Me Now,
Baby, I Don't Care*   RCA EPA 4114

| 1958 | *King Creole, New Orleans, As Long As I Have You, Lover Doll* | RCA EPA 4319 |

1958   King Creole, Vol. 2
Trouble, Young Dreams, Crawfish, Dixieland Rock   RCA EPA 4321

1958   Elvis Sails
Press interview with Elvis Presley at the Brooklyn Army Terminal
(September 22, 1958)   RCA EPA 4325

1958   Christmas with Elvis
White Christmas, Here Comes Santa Claus, O Little Town of Bethlehem,
Silent Night   RCA EPA 4340

1959   A Touch of Gold, Vol. 1
Hard Headed Woman, Good Rockin' Tonight, Don't, I Beg of You   RCA EPA 5088

1959   A Touch of Gold, Vol. 2
Wear My Ring Around Your Neck, Treat Me Nice, One Night,
That's All Right (Mama)   RCA EPA 5101

1960   A Touch of Gold, Vol. 3
Blue Moon of Kentucky, All Shook Up, Don't Ask Me Why, Too Much   RCA EPA 5141

1962   Follow that Dream
Follow that Dream, What a Wonderful Life, Angel, I'm Not the Marrying Kind
RCA EPA 4368

1962   Kid Galahad
This Is Living, I Got Lucky, A Whistling Tune, King of the Whole Wide World,
Riding the Rainbow, Home Is Where the Heart Is   RCA EPA 4371

1964   Viva Las Vegas
If You Think I Don't Need You, I Need Somebody to Lean On, C'mon Everybody,
Tomorrow and Forever   RCA EPA 4382

1965   Tickle Me
I Feel that I've Known You Forever, Slowly But Surely, Night Rider, Dirty,
Dirty Feeling, Put the Blame on Me   RCA EPA 4383

1967   Easy Come, Easy Go
Easy Come, Easy Go, The Love Machine, Yoga Is As Yoga Does, You Gotta Stop,
Sing, You Children, I'll Take Love   RCA EPA 4387

Albums

R.C.A.

**April
1956** Elvis Presley
*Blue Suede Shoes, I'm Counting on You, I Got a Woman, One-Sided Love Affair,
I Love You Because, Just Because, Tutti Frutti, Tryin' to Get to You, I'm Gonna
Sit Right Down and Cry, I'll Never Let You Go, Blue Moon, Money Honey*
RCA LSP 1254

**October
1956** Elvis
*Rip It Up, Love Me, When My Blue Moon Turns to Gold Again, Long Tall Sally,
First in Line, Paralyzed, So Glad You're Mine, Old Shep, Ready Teddy, Anyplace
Is Paradise, How's the World Treating You, How Do You Think I Feel* RCA LSP 1382

**July
1957** Loving You
*From the film: Mean Woman Blues, Teddy Bear, Loving You, Got A Lot o' Lovin'
to Do, Lonesome Cowboy, Hot Dog, Party,* Bonus Songs: *Blueberry Hill, True
Love, Don't Leave Me Now, Have I Told You Lately That I Love You, I Need You So*
RCA LSP 1515

**November
1957** Elvis' Christmas Album
*Santa Claus Is Back in Town, White Christmas, Here Comes Santa Claus, I'll Be
Home for Christmas, Blue Christmas, Santa Bring My Baby Back, O Little Town
of Bethlehem, Silent Night, Peace in the Valley, Believe, Take My Hand,
Precious Lord, It Is No Secret* RCA LSP 1035

**March
1958** Elvis' Golden Records
*Hound Dog, Loving You, All Shook Up, Heartbreak Hotel, Jailhouse Rock, Love
Me, Too Much, Don't Be Cruel, That's When Your Heartaches Begin, Teddy Bear,
Love Me Tender, Treat Me Nice, Any Way You Want Me, I Want You, I Need You,
I Love You* RCA LSP 1707

**August
1958** King Creole
*King Creole, As Long As I Have You, Hard Headed Woman, Trouble, Dixieland
Rock, Don't Ask Me Why, Lover Doll, Crawfish, Young Dreams, Steadfast, Loyal
and True, New Orleans* RCA LSP 1884

February

1959   For LP Fans Only

That's All Right, Lawdy, Miss Clawdy, Mystery Train, Poor Boy, Playing for Keeps, My Baby Left Me, I Was the One, Shake, Rattle and Roll, You're a Heartbreaker, I'm Left, You're Right, She's Gone   RCA LSP 1990

August

1959   A Date with Elvis

Blue Moon of Kentucky, Young and Beautiful, Baby, I Don't Care, Milkcow Blues Boogie, Baby, Let's Play House, Good Rockin' Tonight, Is It So Strange, We're Gonna Move, I Want to Be Free, I Forgot to Remember to Forget   RCA LSP 2011

December

1959   50,000,000 Elvis Fans Can't Be Wrong

Elvis' Gold Records, Vol. 2

A Fool Such As I, I Need Your Love Tonight, Wear My Ring Around Your Neck, Doncha' Think It's Time, I Beg of You, A Big Hunk o' Love, Don't, My Wish Came True, One Night, I Got Stung   RCA LSP 2075

April

1960   Elvis Is Back

Fever, Girl Next Door Went-A-Walking, Soldier Boy, Make Me Know It, I Will Be Home Again, Reconsider, Baby, It Feels So Right, Like a Baby, The Girl of My Best Friend, Thrill of Your Love, Such a Night, Dirty, Dirty Feeling   RCA LSP 2231

October

1960   G. I. Blues

Tonight Is So Right For Love, What's She Really Like, Frankfurt Special, Wooden Heart, G.I. Blues, Pocketful of Rainbows, Shoppin' Around, Big Boots, Didja' Ever, Blue Suede Shoes, Doin' the Best I Can   RCA LSP 2256

December

1960   His Hand in Mine

His Hand In Mine, I'm Gonna Walk Dem Golden Stairs, In My Father's House, Milky White Way, Known Only to Him, I Believe in the Man in the Sky, Joshua Fit the Battle, Jesus Knows What I Need, Swing Down, Sweet Chariot, Mansion over the Hilltop, If We Never Meet Again, Working on the Building   RCA LSP 2328

June

1961   Something for Everybody

The Ballad Side: There's Always Me, Give Me the Right, It's a Sin, Sentimental Me, Starting Today, Gently, The Rhythm Side: I'm Comin' Home, In Your Arms, Put the Blame on Me, Judy, I Want You with Me; Bonus Songs: I Slipped, I Stumbled, I Fell (from Wild in the Country)   RCA LSP 2370

October
1961   Blue Hawaii
*Blue Hawaii, Almost Always True, Aloha Oe, No More, Can't Help Falling in Love,
Rock-a-Hula Baby, Moonlight Swim, Ku-u-i-po, Ito Eats, Slicin' Sand, Hawaiian
Wedding Song*   RCA LSP 2436

June
1962   Pot Luck
*Kiss Me Quick, Just for Old Times' Sake, Gonna Get Back Home Somehow, Easy
Question, Steppin' Out of Line (from* Blue Hawaii*), I'm Yours, Something Blue,
Suspicion, I Feel That I've Known You Forever, Night Rider, Fountain of Love,
That's Someone You Never Forget*   RCA LSP 2523

November
1962   Girls! Girls! Girls!
*Girls! Girls! Girls!, I Don't Wanna Be Tied, Where Do You Come From, I Don't
Want To, We'll Be Together, A Boy Like Me, a Girl Like You, Earth Boy, Return to
Sender, Because of Love, Thanks to the Rolling Sea, Song of the Shrimp, The
Walls Have Ears, We're Coming in Loaded*   RCA LSP 2621

March
1963   It Happened at the World's Fair
*Beyond the Bend, Relax, Take Me to the Fair, They Remind Me Too Much of You,
One Broken Heart for Sale, I'm Falling in Love Tonight, Cotton Candy Land,
A World of Our Own, How Would You Like to Be, Happy Ending*   RCA LSP 2697

September
1963   Elvis' Golden Records, Vol. 3
*It's Now or Never, Stuck on You, Fame and Fortune, I Gotta Know, Surrender,
I Feel So Bad, Are You Lonesome Tonight, His Latest Flame, Little Sister,
Good Luck Charm, Anything That's Part of You, She's Not You*   RCA LSP 2765

November
1963   Fun in Acapulco
*Fun in Acapulco, Vino, Dinero y Amor, Mexico, El Toro, Marguerita, The
Bullfighter Was a Lady, No Room to Rhumba in a Sports Car, I Think I'm Gonna
Like It Here, Bossa Nova Baby, You Can't Say No in Acapulco, Guadalajara;
Bonus Songs: Love Me Tonight, Slowly But Surely*   RCA LSP 2756

March
1964   Kissin' Cousins
*Kissin' Cousins, Smokey Mountain Boy, There's Gold in the Mountains, One Boy,
Two Little Girls, Catchin' On Fast, Tender Feeling, Anyone, Barefoot Ballad,
Once Is Enough; Bonus Songs: Echoes of Love, Long, Lonely Highway* RCA LSP 2894

October
1964   Roustabout
Roustabout, Little Egypt, Poison Ivy League, Hard Knocks, It's a Wonderful World, Big Love, Big Heartache, One-Track Heart, It's Carnival Time, Carny Town, There's a Brand New Day on the Horizon, Wheels on My Heels   RCA LSP 2999

April
1965   Girl Happy
Girl Happy, Spring Fever, Fort Lauderdale Chamber of Commerce, Startin' Tonight, Wolf Call, Do Not Disturb, Cross My Heart and Hope to Die, The Meanest Girl in Town, Do the Clam, Puppet on a String, I've Got to Find My Baby; Bonus Song: You'll Be Gone   RCA LSP 3338

July
1965   Elvis for Everyone
Your Cheatin' Heart, Summer Kisses, Winter Tears, Finders Keepers, Losers Weepers, In My Way (from Wild in the Country*), Tomorrow Night, Memphis, Tennessee, For the Millionth and the Last Time, Forget Me Never (from* Wild in the Country*), Sound Advice (from* Follow That Dream*), Santa Lucia (from* Viva Las Vegas*), I Met Her Today, When It Rains, It Really Pours*   RCA LSP 3450

October
1965   Harum Scarum
Harem Holiday, My Desert Serenade, Go East—Young Man, Mirage, Kismet, Shake That Tambourine, Hey Little Girl, Golden Coins, So Close, Yet So Far; Bonus Songs: Animal Instinct, Wisdom of the Ages   RCA LSP 3468

April
1966   Frankie and Johnny
Frankie and Johnny, Come Along, Petunia, the Gardener's Daughter, Chesay, What Every Woman Lives For, Look Out, Broadway, Beginner's Luck, Down by the Riverside and When the Saints Go Marching In (medley), Shout It Out, Hard Luck, Please Don't Stop Loving Me, Everybody Come Aboard   RCA LSP 3553

June
1966   Paradise; Hawaiian Style
Paradise; Hawaiian Style, Queenie Wahine's Papaya, Scratch My Back, Drums of the Islands, Datin', A Dog's Life, House of Sand, Stop Where You Are, This Is My Heaven; Bonus Song: Sand Castles   RCA LSP 3643

October
1966   Spinout
Stop, Look and Listen, Adam and Evil, All That I Am, Never Say Yes, Am I Ready, Beach Shack, Spinout, Smorgasbord, I'll Be Back; Bonus Songs: Tomorrow Is a Long Time, Down in the Alley, I'll Remember You   RCA LSP 3702

March

1967 How Great Thou Art

How Great Thou Art, In the Garden, Somebody Bigger Than You and I, Farther Along, Stand by Me, Without Him, So High, Where Could I Go But to the Lord, By and By, If the Lord Wasn't Walking by My Side, Run On, Where No One Stands Alone, Crying in the Chapel RCA LSP 3758

June

1967 Double Trouble

Double Trouble, Baby, If You'll Give Me All of Your Love, Could I Fall in Love, Long Legged Girl, City by Night, Old MacDonald, I Love Only One Girl, There Is So Much World to See; Bonus Songs: *It Won't Be Long, Never Ending, Blue River, What Now, What Next, Where To* RCA LSP 3787

November

1967 Clambake

Clambake, Who Needs Money, A House That Has Everything, Confidence, Hey, Hey, Hey, You Don't Know Me, The Girl I Never Loved; Bonus Songs: Guitar Man, How Can You Lose What You Never Had, Big Boss Man, Singing Tree, Just Call Me Lonesome RCA LSP 3893

February

1968 Elvis' Gold Records, Vol. 4

Love Letters, Witchcraft, It Hurts Me, What'd I Say, Please Don't Drag That String Around, Indescribably Blue, You're the Devil in Disguise, Lonely Man, A Mess of Blues, Ask Me, Ain't That Loving You, Baby, Just Tell Her Jim Said Hello RCA LSP 3921

June

1968 Speedway

Speedway, There Ain't Nothing Like a Song (with Nancy Sinatra), Your Time Hasn't Come Yet Baby, Who Are You, He's Your Uncle, Not Your Dad, Let Yourself Go, Your Groovy Self (with Nancy Sinatra); Bonus Songs: *Five Sleepy Heads, Western Union, Mine, Goin' Home, Suppose* RCA LSP 3989

November

1968 Elvis Singing Flaming Star and Others

Flaming Star (from Flaming Star), *Wonderful World (from* Live a Little, Love a Little), *Night Life, All I Needed Was the Rain, Too Much Monkey Business, Yellow Rose of Texas and The Eyes of Texas (medley), She's a Machine, Do the Vega, Tiger Man (recorded live at NBC for the Elvis special, for which this album was released through Singer Sewing Centers)* RCA PRS 279

December
1968 Elvis (TV Special)

Trouble and Guitar Man, Lawdy, Miss Clawdy and Baby, What You Want Me to do, Dialogue, Medley: Heartbreak Hotel, Hound Dog, All Shook Up, Can't Help Falling in Love, Jailhouse Rock, Dialogue, Love Me Tender, Dialogue, Where Could I go But to the Lord, Up Above My Head and Saved, Dialogue, Blue Christmas, Dialogue, One Night, Memories, Medley: Nothingville, Dialogue, Big Boss Man, Guitar Man, Little Egypt, Trouble, Guitar Man, If I Can Dream

RCA LPM 4088

May
1969 From Elvis in Memphis

Wearin' That Loved On Look, Only the Strong Survive, I'll Hold You in My Heart, Long Black Limousine, It Keeps Right on A-Hurtin', I'm Movin' On, Power of My Love, Gentle on My Mind, After Loving You, True Love Travels on a Gravel Road, Any Day Now, In the Ghetto

RCA LSP 4155

November
1969 From Memphis to Vegas / From Vegas to Memphis (2-record set)

Blue Suede Shoes, Johnny B. Goode, All Shook Up, Are You Lonesome Tonight, Hound Dog, I Can't Stop Loving You, My Babe, Mystery Train and Tiger Man (medley), Words, In the Ghetto, Suspicious Minds, Can't Help Falling in Love, Inherit the Wind, This is the Story, Stranger in My Own Home Town, A Little Bit of Green, And the Grass Won't Pay No Mind, Do You Know Who I Am, From a Jack to a King, The Fair's Moving On, You'll Think of Me, Without Love

RCA LSP 6020

May
1970 On Stage: February, 1970

See See Rider, Release Me, Sweet Caroline, Run-away, The Wonder of You, Polk Salad Annie, Yesterday, Proud Mary, Walk a Mile in My Shoes, Let It Be Me

RCA LSP 4362

August
1970 Worldwide 50 Gold Award Hits, Vol. 1.

Heartbreak Hotel, I Was the One, I Want You, I Need You, I Love You, Don't Be Cruel, Hound Dog, Love Me Tender, Any Way You Want Me, Too Much, Playing for Keeps, All Shook Up, That's When Your Heartaches Begin, Loving You, Teddy Bear, Jailhouse Rock, Trust Me Nice, I Beg of You, Don't, Wear My Ring Around Your Neck, Hard Headed Woman, I Got Stung, A Fool Such As I, A Big Hunk o'Love, Stuck on You, A Mess of Blues, It's Now or Never, I Gotta Know, Are You Lonesome Tonight, Surrender, I Feel So Bad, Little Sister, Can't Help Falling in Love, Rock-a-Hula Baby, Anything That's Part of You, Good Luck Charm, She's Not You, Return to Sender, Where Do You Come From, One

Broken Heart for Sale, Devil in Disguise, Bossa Nova Baby, Kissin' Cousins, Viva Las Vegas, Ain't That Loving You, Baby, Wooden Heart, Crying in the Chapel, If I Can Dream, In the Ghetto, Suspicious Minds, Don't Cry, Daddy, Kentucky Rain; Plus: Excerpts from Elvis Sails   RCA LPM 6401

November
1970   Back in Memphis
Inherit the Wind, This Is the Story, Stranger in My Own Home Town, A Little Bit of Green, The Grass Won't Pay No Mind, Do You Know Who I Am, From a Jack to a King, The Fair's Moving On, You'll Think of Me, Without Love   RCA LSP 4429

December
1970   Elvis: That's the Way It Is
I Just Can't Help Believin', Twenty Days and Twenty Nights, How the Web Was Woven, Patch It Up, Mary in the Morning, You Don't Have to Say You Love Me, You've Lost That Lovin' Feeling, I've Lost Me, You've Lost That Lovin' Feeling, I've Lost You, Just Pretend, Stranger in the Crowd, The Next Step Is Love, Bridge Over Troubled Water   RCA LSP 4445

September
1971   Elvis: The Other Sides—Worldwide Gold Award Hits, Vol. 2
Puppet on a String, Witchcraft, Trouble, Poor Boy, I Want To Be Free, Doncha' Think It's Time, Young Dreams, The Next Step Is Love, You Don't Have to Say You Love Me, Paralyzed, My Wish Came True, When My Blue Moon Turns to Gold Again, Lonesome Cowboy, My Baby Left Me, It Hurts Me, I Need Your Love Tonight, Tell Me Why, Please Don't Drag That String Around, Young and Beautiful, Hot Dog, New Orleans, We're Gonna Move, Crawfish, King Creole, I Believe In the Man in the Sky, Dixieland Rock, The Wonder of You, They Remind Me Too Much of You, Mean Woman Blues, Lonely Man, Any Day Now, Don't Ask My Why, Marie's the Name—His Latest Flame, I Really Don't Want to Know, (You're So Square) Baby I Don't Care, I've Lost You, Let Me, Love Me, Got a Lot o' Living to Do, Fame and Fortune, Rip It Up, There Goes My Everything, Lover Doll, One Night, Just Tell Her Jim Said Hello, Ask Me, Patch It Up, As Long As I Have You, You'll Think of Me, Wild in the Country   RCA LPM 6402

December
1971   The Wonderful World of Christmas
O Come, All Ye Faithful, The First Noel, Winter Wonderland, Silver Bells, On a Snowy Christmas Night, It Won't Seem Like Christmas, I'll Be Home on Christmas Day, Holly Leaves and Christmas Trees, Merry Christmas Baby, If I Get Home on Christmas Day, The Wonderful World of Christmas   RCA LSP 4579

**March
1971**   Elvis Country

*Snowbird, Tomorrow Never Comes, Little Cabin on the Hill, Whole Lot-ta Shakin'
Goin' On, Funny How Time Slips Away, I Really Don't Want to Know, There Goes
My Everything, It's Your Baby, You Rock It, The Fool, Faded Love, I Washed My
Hands in Muddy Water, Make the World Go Away, I Was Born About Ten
Thousand Years Ago*   RCA LSP 4460

**August
1971**   Love Letters from Elvis

*Love Letters, When I'm Over You, If I Were You, Got My Mojo Working, Heart of
Rome, Only Believe, This Is Our Dance, Cindy, Cindy, I'll Never Know, Life,
It Ain't No Big Thing*   RCA LSP 4530

**March
1972**   Elvis—Now

*Help Me Make It Through the Night, Miracle of the Rosary, Hey Jude, Put Your
Hand in the Hand, Until It's Time for You to Go, We Can Make the Morning,
Early Mornin' Rain, Sylvia, Fools Rush In, I Was Born Ten Thousand Years Ago*
                                                                       RCA LSP 4671

**June
1972**   He Touched Me

*He Touched Me, I've Got Confidence, Amazing Grace, Seeing Is Believing, He Is
My Everything, Bosom of Abraham, An Evening Prayer, Lead Me, Guide Me,
There Is No God But God, A Thing Called Love, I, John, Reach Out to Jesus*
                                                                       RCA LSP 4690

**August
1972**   Elvis As Recorded Live at Madison Square Garden (June 10, 1972)

*Introduction: Also sprach Zarathustra, That's All Right, Proud Mary, Never Been
to Spain, You Don't Have to Say You Love Me, You've Lost that Lovin' Feelin,
Polk Salad Annie, Love Me, All Shook Up, Heartbreak Hotel, Medley: (Let Me Be
Your) Teddy Bear and Don't Be Cruel, Love Me Tender, The Impossible Dream,
Introductions by Elvis, Hound Dog, Suspicious Minds, For the Good Times,
American Trilogy, Funny How Time Slips Away, I Can't Stop Loving You, Can't
Help Falling in Love*   RCA LSP 4776

**April
1973**   Aloha from Hawaii Via Satellite (January 14, 1973)

*Introduction: Also sprach Zarathustra, See See Rider, Burning Love, Something,
You Gave Me a Mountain, Steamroller Blues, My Way, Love Me, Johnny B.
Goode, It's Over, Blue Suede Shoes, I'm So Lonesome I Could Cry, I Can't Stop
Loving You, Hound Dog, What Now My Love, Fever, Welcome to My World,
Suspicious Minds, Introductions by Elvis, I'll Remember You, Medley: Long Tall*

Sally and Whole Lot-ta Shakin' Goin' On, American Trilogy, A Big Hunk o' Love,
Can't Help Falling in Love RCA VPSX-6089

July
1973 ELVIS
Fool, Where Do I Go From Here, It's Impossible, It's Still Here, I Will Be True,
I'll Take You Home Again Kathleen, (That's What You Get) For Lovin' Me, Padre,
Don't Think Twice, It's All Right, Love Me, Love the Life I Lead RCA APL 1-0283

October
1973 Raised On Rock/For Ol' Times Sake
Raised on Rock, Are You Sincere, Find Out What's Happening, I Miss You, Girl of
Mine, For Ol' Times Sake, If You Don't Come Back, Just a Little Bit, Sweet
Angeline, Three Corn Patches RCA APL 1-0388

January
1974 ELVIS: A Legendary Performer, Vol. 1
That's All Right, I Love You Because (unreleased take), *Heartbreak Hotel, Don't*
Be Cruel, Love Me (unreleased live version), *Trying To Get To You* (unreleased
live version), *Love Me Tender, (There'll Be) Peace In the Valley, (Now and Then*
There's) A Fool Such As I, Tonight's All Right for Love (unreleased song from
G.I. Blues), *Are You Lonesome Tonight?* (unreleased live version), *Can't Help*
Falling in Love, plus excerpts from Elvis' press conference on September 22,
1958. RCA CPL 1-0341

May
1974 Good Times
Take Good Care of Her, Loving Arms, I Got a Feelin' in My Body, If That Isn't
Love, She Wears My Ring, I've Got a Thing About You Baby, My Boy, Spanish
Eyes, Talk About the Good Times, Good Time Charlie's Got the Blues
RCA CPL 1-0475

September
1974 Elvis As Recorded Live On Stage in Memphis
See See Rider, I Got a Woman, Love Me. Trying to Get to You, Medley: Long Tall
Sally, Whole Lot-Ta Shakin' Goin On, Flip, Flop and Fly, Jailhouse Rock and
Hound Dog, Why Me Lord, How Great Thou Art, Medley: Blueberry Hill and I
Can't Stop Loving You, Help Me, An American Trilogy, Let Me Be There, My Baby
Left Me, Lawdy, Miss Clawdy, Can't Help Falling in Love RCA CPL 1-0606

October
1974 Having Fun with Elvis on Stage
A Talking Album only—Elvis talking to and with his concert audiences (Album
was privately recorded and marketed briefly before RCA bought up the rights)
RCA CPM 1-0818

January
1975   Promised Land
          *Promised Land, There's A Honky Tonk Angel (Who Will Take Me Back In), Help
          Me, Mr. Songman, Love Song of the Year, It's Midnight, Your Love's Been a Long
          Time Coming, If You Talk in Your Sleep, Thinking About You, You Asked Me To*
                                                                    RCA APL 1-0873

January
1976   ELVIS: A Legendary Performer, Vol. 2
          *Harbor Lights (unreleased Sun recording), How Great Thou Art, If I Can Dream, I
          Want You, I Need You, I Love You (unreleased alternate take), Blue Christmas, Blue
          Suede Shoes (unreleased live recording), It's Now or Never, Blue Hawaii
          (unreleased live recording), Jailhouse Rock, 1956 interview, Such a Night, Blue
          Hawaii (unreleased live recording), 1961 awards presentation to Elvis, Cane and a
          High Starched Collar (unreleased recording)*   RCA CPL 1-1349

March
1976   ELVIS: The Sun Sessions
          *That's All Right, Blue Moon of Kentucky, I Don't Care If the Sun Don't Shine, Good
          Rockin' Tonight, Milkcow Blues Boogie, You're a Heartbreaker, I'm Left, You're
          Right, She's Gone, Baby Let's Play House, Mystery Train, I Forgot to Remember to
          Forget, I'll Never Let You Go, I Love You Because (first version), I Love You Because
          (second version), Blue Moon, Trying to Get to You, Just Because*   RCA APM 1-1675

May
1976   From Elvis Presley Boulevard, Memphis, Tennessee (Recorded Live)
          *Hurt, Never Again, Blue Eyes Crying in the Rain, Danny Boy, The Last Farewell, For
          the Heart, Better They Are, Harder They Fall, Love Coming Down, I'll Never Fall in
          Love Again*   RCA APL 1-1506

March
1977   Welcome to My World
          *Welcome to My World (live recording), Help Me Make It Through the Night, Release
          Me (And Let Me Love Again) (live recording), I Really Don't Want to Know, For the
          Good Times (live recording), Gentle on My Mind, Make the World Go Away (live
          recording), Your Cheatin' Heart, I'm So Lonesome I Could Cry (live recording), I
          Can't Stop Loving You (previously unreleased live recording)*   RCA APL 1-2274

June
1977   Moody Blue
          *Moody Blue, She Thinks I Still Care, Way Down, Pledging My Love, It's Easy for You,
          Let Me Be There, If You Love Me Let Me Know, He'll Have to Go, Unchained
          Melody, Little Darlin'*   RCA AFL 1-2428

194

CAMDEN

April
1969
Elvis Sings "Flaming Star"
Commercial release of the Presley album (RCA PRS-279) issued as a special
premium in November 1968 in conjunction with the Singer TV program.

RCA CAS-2304

April
1970
Let's Be Friends
Stay Away, Joe (from Stay Away Joe*), If I'm a Fool, Let's Be Friends, Let's Forget
About the Stars, Mama (from* Girls! Girls! Girls!*), I'll Be There, Almost (from*
The Trouble with Girls*), Change of Habit (from* Change of Habit*), Have a Happy
(from* Change of Habit*)*

RCA CAS-2408

November
1970
Elvis' Christmas Album
*Blue Christmas, Silent Night, White Christmas, Santa Claus Is Back in Town,
I'll Be Home for Christmas, If Every Day Was Like Christmas, Here Comes Santa
Claus, O Little Town of Bethlehem, Santa Bring My Baby Back, Mama Liked the
Roses*

RCA CAL-2428

November
1970
Almost in Love
Almost in Love (from Live a Little, Love a Little*), Long Legged Girl (from* Double
Trouble*), Edge of Reality (from* Live a Little, Love a Little*), My Little Friend, A
Little Less Conversation (from* Live a Little, Love a Little*), Rubberneckin' (from*
Change of Habit*), Clean Up Your Own Back Yard (from* The Trouble with Girls*),
U. S. Male (from* Stay Away, Joe*), Charro! (from* Charro!*), Stay Away, Joe (from*
Stay Away, Joe*)*

RCA CAS-2440

March
1971
You'll Never Walk Alone
You'll Never Walk Alone, Who Am I?, Let Us Pray (from Change of Habit*),
(There'll Be) Peace in the Valley, We Call On Him, I Believe, It Is No Secret (What
God Can Do), Sing You Children, Take My Hand, Precious Lord*

RCA CALX-2472

August
1971
C'mon Everybody
*C'mon Everybody, Angel, Easy Come, Easy Go, A Whistling Tune, Follow That
Dream, King of the Whole Wide World, I'll Take Love, Today, Tomorrow and
Forever, I'm Not the Marrying Kind, This Is Living*

RCA CAL-2518

November
1971   I Got Lucky

I Got Lucky (from Kid Galahad), What a Wonderful Life (from Follow That Dream), I Need Somebody to Lean On (from Viva Las Vegas), Yoga Is As Yoga Does (from Easy Come, Easy Go), Riding the Rainbow (from Kid Galahad), Fools Fall in Love, The Love Machine (from Easy Come, Easy Go), Home Is Where the Heart Is (from Kid Galahad), You Gotta Stop (from Easy Come, Easy Go), If You Think I Don't Need You (from Viva Las Vegas)
                                                           RCA CAL-2533

March
1972   Elvis Sings Hits from His Movies, Vol. 1

Down By the Riverside and When the Saints Go Marching In (from Frankie and Johnny), They Remind Me Too Much of You (from It Happened at the World's Fair), Confidence, from Clambake), Frankie and Johnny (from Frankie and Johnny), Guitar Man, Long Legged Girl (With the Short Dress On), from Double Trouble), You Don't Know Me (from Clambake), How Would You Like to Be (from It Happened at the World's Fair), Big Boss Man, Old MacDonald (from Double Trouble)
                                                            RCA CAS-2567

July
1972   "Burning Love" and Hits from His Movies, Vol. 2

Burning Love, Tender Feeling, Am I Ready, Tonight Is So Right for Love, Guadalajara, It's A Matter of Time, No More, Santa Lucia, We'll Be Together, I Love Only One Girl
                                                            RCA CAS-2595

November
1972   Separate Ways

Separate Ways, Sentimental Me, In My Way, I Met Her Today, What Now, What Next, Where To, Always on My Mind, I Slipped, I Stumbled, I Feel, Is It So Strange, Forget Me Never, Old Shep
                                                            RCA CAS-2611

April
1975   Elvis: Pure Gold

Love Me Tender, Loving You, Kentucky Rain, Fever, It's Impossible, Jailhouse Rock, Don't Be Cruel, I Got a Woman, All Shook Up, In the Ghetto
                                                          ANL 1-0971

Elvis Presley Filmography

Love Me Tender
(Twentieth Century-Fox, 1956) 89 min.

CREDITS: Producer, David Weisbart; director, Robert D. Webb; screenplay, Robert Buckner; based on the story *The Reno Brothers* by Maurice Geraghty; photography, Leo Tover; music, Lionel Newman; songs, Elvis Presley and Vera Matson; art direction, Lyle R. Wheeler and Maurice Ransford; set decoration, Walter M. Scott and Fay Babcock; special effects, Ray Kellogg; costumes, Mary Wills; assistant director, Stanley Hough; editor, Hugh S. Fowler. CinemaScope, b&w. (Originally called *The Reno Brothers.*)

CAST: Richard Egan (Vance Reno), Debra Paget (Cathy), Elvis Presley (Clint Reno), Robert Middleton (Siringo), William Campbell (Brett Reno), Neville Brand (Mike Gavin), Mildred Dunnock (The Mother), Bruce Bennett (Maj. Kincaid), James Drury (Ray Reno), Russ Conway (Ed Galt), Ken Clark (Kelso), Barry Coe (Davis), L. Q. Jones (Fleming), Paul Burns (Jethro), Jerry Sheldon (Train Conductor), James Stone (Storekeeper), Ed Mundy (Auctioneer), Joe Di Reda (First Soldier), Bobby Rose (Station Agent), Tom Greenway (Paymaster), Jay Jostyn (Maj. Harris), Steve Darrell (Second Conductor).

SYNOPSIS: Elvis is the younger brother who marries the girlfriend of the brother who is away fighting for the Confederacy.

Jailhouse Rock
(Metro-Goldwyn-Mayer, 1957) 96 min.

CREDITS: An Avon Production. Producer, Pandro S. Berman; associate producer, Katherine Hereford; director, Richard Thorpe; screenplay, Guy Trosper; based on a story by Ned Young; photography, Robert Bronner; music, Jeff Alexander; art direction, William A. Hornung and Randall Duell; set decoration, Henry Grace and Keogh Gleason; special effects, A. Arnold Gillespie; technical advisor, Col. Tom Parker; assistant director, Robert E. Relyea; editor, Ralph E. Winters. CinemaScope.

CAST: Elvis Presley (Vince Everett), Judy Tyler (Peggy Van Alden), Mickey Shaughnessy (Hank Houghton), Vaughn Taylor (Mr. Shores), Jennifer Holden (Sherry Wilson), Dean Jones (Teddy Talbot), Anne Neyland (Laury Jackson), Grandon Rhodes (Prof. August Van Alden), Katherine Warren (Mrs. Van Alden), Don Burnett (Mickey Alba), George Cisar (Jake the Bartender), Hugh Sanders (Warden), Glenn Strange (Convict), John Indrisano (Convict), Robert Bice (Bardeman), Percy

Helton (Sam Brewster), Peter Adams (Jack Lease), William Forrest (Studio Head), Dan White (Paymaster), Robin Raymond (Dotty), John Day (Ken), S. John Launer (Judge), Dick Rich (Guard), Elizabeth Slifer (Cleaning Woman), Gloria Paul (Stripper), Fred Coby (Bartender), Walter Johnson (Shorty), Frank Kreig (Drunk), William Tannen (Record Distributor), Wilson Wood (Recording Engineer), Tom McKee (TV Director), Donald Kerr (Photographer), Carl Milletaire (Drummond), Francis DeSales (Surgeon), Harry Hines (Hotel Clerk), Dorothy Abbott (Extra in Café), The Jordanaires (Themselves).

SYNOPSIS: Elvis is an itinerant shovel-driver who goes from jail on a manslaughter rap to stardom as a recording artist.

Loving You
(Paramount, 1957) 101 min.

CREDITS: A Hal Wallis Production. Producer, Hal B. Wallis; associate producer, Paul Nathan; director, Hal Kantor; screenplay, Herbert Baker; based on the *Good Housekeeping* story *A Call from Mitch Miller* by Mary Agnes Thompson; photography, Charles Lang, Jr.; music, Walter Scharf; choreography, Charles O'Curran; art direction, Hal Pereira and Albert Nozaki; set decoration, Sam Comer and Frank McKelvy; special effects, John P. Fulton; costumes, Edith Head; technical advisor, Col. Tom Parker; editor, Howard Smith. VistaVision, Technicolor. (Originally called *Something for the Girls* and *The Lonesome Cowboy*.)

CAST: Elvis Presley (Deke Rivers), Lizabeth Scott (Glenda Markle), Wendell Corey (Walker ''Tex'' Warner), Dolores Hart (Susan Jessup), James Gleason (Carl Meade), Paul Smith (Skeeter), Ken Becker (Wayne), Jana Lund (Daisy), Ralph Dumke (Tallman), Yvonne Lime (Sally), Skip Young (Teddy), Vernon Rich (Harry Taylor), David Cameron (Castle), Grace Hayle (Mrs. Gunderson), Dick Ryan (Mack), Steve Pendleton (O'Shea), Sydney Chatton (Grew), Jack Latham (TV Announcer), William Forrest (Mr. Jessup), Irene Tedrow (Mrs. Jessup), Hal K. Dawson (Lieutenant), Madge Blake (Woman), Joe Forte (Editor), Almira Sessions (Woman), Karen Scott (Waitress), Beach Dickerson (Glenn), Gail Lund (Candy), Harry Cheshire (Mayor), Timothy Butler (Buzz), Myrna Fahey (Girl), Sue England (Sorority Girl), The Jordanaires (Themselves), Gladys Presley (Extra in Audience), Vernon Presley (Man).

SYNOPSIS: Elvis is a hillbilly singer who is guided to success in the big city by a crafty lady press agent.

King Creole
(Paramount, 1958) 116 min.

CREDITS: A Hal Wallis Production. Producer, Hal B. Wallis; associate producer,

Paul Nathan; director, Michael Curtiz; screenplay, Herbert Baker and Michael V. Gazzo; based on the novel *A Stone for Danny Fisher* by Harold Robbins; photography, Russell Harlan; music, Walter Scharf; choreography, Charles O'Curran; art direction, Hal Pereira and Joseph MacMillan Johnson; set decoration, Sam Comer and Frank McKelvy; special effects, John P. Fulton; costumes, Edith Head; technical advisor, Col. Tom Parker; assistant director, D. Michael Moore; editor, Warren Low. VistaVision. (Filmed in New Orleans and originally called *Sing, You Sinner.*)

CAST: Elvis Presley (Danny Fisher), Carolyn Jones (Bonnie), Dolores Hart (Nellie), Dean Jagger (Mr. Fisher), Walter Matthau (Maxie Fields), Liliane Montevecchi ("Forty" Nina), Vic Morrow (Shark), Jan Shepard (Mimi Fisher), Paul Stewart (Charlie LeGrand), Brian Hutton (Sal), Jack Grinnage (Dummy), Dick Winslow (Eddie Burton), Raymond Bailey (Mr. Evans), Ziva Rodann (Chorus Girl), Ned Glass (Desk Clerk), Candy Candido (Doorman), Lilyan Chauvin (Girl), Franklyn Farnum (Old Man), Minta Durfee (Old Woman), Hazel "Sonny" Boyne (Old Woman), The Jordanaires (Themselves).

SYNOPSIS: Elvis is a downtrodden musician in New Orleans who becomes entangled with gangster kingpin Matthau and his associates.

Flaming Star
(Twentieth Century-Fox, 1960) 101 min.

CREDITS: Producer, David Weisbart; director, Don Siegel; screenplay, Clair Huffaker and Nunnally Johnson; based on a novel, *Flaming Lance,* by Huffaker; photography, Charles G. Clarke; music, Cyril Mockridge; conducted by Lionel Newman; choreography, Josephine Earl; art direction, Duncan Cramer and Walter M. Simonds; set decoration, Walter M. Scott and Gustav Bernsten; costumes, Adele Balkan; assistant director, Joseph E. Rickards; 2nd unit director, Richard Talmadge; editor, Hugh S. Fowler. CinemaScope and De Luxe Color. (Originally called *Flaming Heart* and *Black Star.*)

CAST: Elvis Presley (Pacer Burton), Barbara Eden (Roslyn Pierce), Steve Forrest (Clint Burton), Dolores Del Rio (Neddy Burton), John McIntire (Pa Burton), Rudolfo Acosta (Buffalo Horn), Karl Swenson (Dred Pierce), Ford Rainey (Doc Phillips), Richard Jaeckel (Angus Pierce), Anne Benton (Dorothy Howard), L. Q. Jones (Tom Howard), Douglas Dick (Will Howard), Tom Reese (Jute), Marian Goldina (Ph'Sha Knay), Monty Burkhardt (Ben Ford), Ted Jacques (Hornsby), Roy Jenson (Matt Holcom), Barbara Beaird (Dottie Phillips), Virginia Christine (Mrs. Phillips), Rodd Redwing (Indian Brave), Perry Lopez (Two Moons), Sharon Bercutt (Bird's Wing), Tom Fadden (Townsman), The Jordanaires (Themselves).

SYNOPSIS: Elvis is a half-breed caught up in the bloody strife between the settlers and the Indians in Texas.

G.I. Blues
(Paramount, 1960) 104 min.

CREDITS: A Hal Wallis Production. Producer, Hal B. Wallis; associate producer, Paul Nathan; director, Norman Taurog; screenplay, Edmund Beloin and Henry Garson; photography, Loyal Griggs; music, Joseph J. Lilley; choreography, Charles O'Curran; art direction, Walter Tyler; set decoration, Sam Comer and Ray Mayer; special effects, John P. Fulton; costumes, Edith Head; technical advisor, Col. Tom Parker; assistant director, D. Michael Moore; editor, Warren Low. Technicolor.

CAST: Elvis Presley (Tulsa McCauley), Juliet Prowse (Lili), Robert Ivers (Cookie), Leticia Roman (Tina), James Douglas (Rick), Sigrid Maier (Marla), Arch Johnson (Sgt. McGraw), Mickey Knox (Jeeter), John Hudson (Capt. Hobart), Ken Becker (Mac), Jeremy Slate (Turk), Beach Dickerson (Warren), Trent Dolan (Mickey), Carl Crow (Walt), Fred Essler (Papa Mueller), Ronald Starr (Harvey), Erika Peters (Trudy), Ludwig Stossel (Puppet Show Owner), Robert Boon (German Guitarist), Edith Angold (Mrs. Hagermann), Dick Winslow (Orchestra Leader), Ed Faulkner (Red), Edward Coch (Band Leader), Fred Kruger (Herr Klugmann), Torben Meyer (Headwaiter), Gene Roth (First Businessman), Roy C. Wright (Second Businessman), Harper Carter (M.P.), Tip McClure (M.P.), Walter Conrad (Chaplain), Edward Stroll (Dynamite), William Kaufman (Kaffeehouse Manager), Hannarl Melcher (Strolling Girl Singer), Elisha Matthew "Bitsy" Mott, Jr. (Sergeant), Judith Rawlins (Fritzie), Blaine Turner (Bartender), Marianne Gaba (Bargirl), Britta Ekman (Redhead), The Jordanaires (Themselves).

SYNOPSIS: Guitar-playing Elvis is a tank gunner with the U.S. Army in Germany. After his military hitch, he and his buddies plan to open a nightclub. Prowse is the cabaret dancer he woos on a bait and with whom he falls in love.

Blue Hawaii
(Paramount, 1961) 101 min.

CREDITS: A Hal Wallis Production. Producer, Hal B. Wallis; associate producer, Paul Nathan; director, Norman Taurog; screenplay, Hal Kanter; based on the story *Beach Boy* by Allan Weiss; photography, Charles Lang, Jr.; music, Joseph J. Lilley; choreography, Charles O'Curran; art direction, Hal Pereira and Walter Tyler; set decoration, Sam Comer and Frank McKelvy; special effects, John P. Fulton; costumes, Edith Head; technical advisor, Col. Tom Parker; assistant director, D. Michael Moore; editors, Warren Low and Terry Morse. Panavision and Technicolor.

CAST: Elvis Presley (Chad Gates), Joan Blackman (Maile Duval), Nancy Walters (Abigail Prentace), Roland Winters (Fred Gates), Angela Lansbury (Sarah Lee Gates), John Archer (Jack Kelman), Howard McNear (Mr. Chapman), Flora Hayes (Mrs. Manaka), Gregory Gay (Mr. Duval), Steve Brodie (Tucker Garvey), Iris Adrian (Enid Garvey), Darlene Tompkins (Patsy), Pamela Akert (Sandy), Christian Kay

(Beverly), Jenny Maxwell (Ellie Corbett), Frank Atienza (Ito O'Hara), Lani Kai (Carl), Jose De Vega (Ernie), Ralph "Tiki" Hanalie (Wes), Hilo Hattie (Waihila), Richard Reeves (Convict), Michael Ross (Lt. Grey), The Jordanaires (Themselves).

SYNOPSIS: Elvis is an ex-G.I. who becomes a tour guide in Hawaii to elude his rich, domineering parents (Lansbury and Winters).

Wild in the Country
(Twentieth Century-Fox, 1961) 114 min.

CREDITS: Producer, Jerry Wald; director, Philip Dunne; screenplay, Clifford Odets; based on the novel *The Lost Country* by J. R. Salamanca; photography, William C. Mellor; music, Kenyon Hopkins; art direction, Jack Martin Smith and Preston Ames; set decoration, Walter M. Scott and Stuart A. Reiss; costumes, Don Feld; assistant director, Joseph E. Rickards; editor, Dorothy Spencer. CinemaScope and De Luxe Color.

CAST: Elvis Presley (Glenn Tyler), Hope Lange (Irene Sperry), Tuesday Weld (Noreen), Millie Perkins (Betty Lee Parsons), Rafer Johnson (Davis), John Ireland (Phil Macy), Gary Lockwood (Cliff Macy), William Mims (Uncle Rolfe), Raymond Greenleaf (Dr. Underwood), Christina Crawford (Monica George), Robin Raymond (Flossie), Doreen Lang (Mrs. Parsons), Charles Arnt (Mr. Parsons), Ruby Goodwin (Sarah), Will Corry (Willie Dace), Alan Napier (Professor Larson), Jason Robards, Sr. (Judge Parker), Harry Carter (Bartender), Harry Sherman (Sam Tyler), Bobby West (Hank Tyler), Elisha M. Mott (State Trooper), Walter Baldwin (Spangler), Mike Lally (Huckster), Joe Butham (Mr. Dace), Hans Moebus (Conductor), Linden Chiles, Jr. (Doctor), Jack Orrison (Coroner).

SYNOPSIS: Presley plays a rebellious country youth who is saved from delinquency and convinced to put his writing talents to use by psychiatrist Hope Lange.

Follow That Dream
(United Artists, 1962) 109 min.

CREDITS: A Mirisch Company Production. Producer, David Weisbart; director, Gordon Douglas; screenplay, Charles Lederer; based on the novel *Pioneer, Go Home!* by Richard Powell; photography, Leo Tover; music, Hans J. Salter; art direction, Malcolm Bert; set decoration, Gordon Gurnee and Fred McClean; assistant director, Bert Chervin; editor, William B. Murphy. Panavision and De Luxe Color.

CAST: Elvis Presley (Toby Kwimper), Arthur O'Connell (Pop Kwimper), Ann Helm (Holly Jones), Joanna Moore (Alicia Claypoole), Jack Kruschen (Carmine), Simon Oakland (Nick), Herbert Rudley (Endicott), Roland Winters (Judge), Alan Hewitt (H. Arthur King), Howard McNear (George), Frank De Kova (Jack), Harry Holcombe

(Governor), Gavin Koon (Eddy Bascombe), Robert Koon (Teddy Bascombe), Pam Ogles (Ariadne Pennington), Robert Carricart (Al), John Duke (Blackie).

SYNOPSIS: Elvis is the spokesman for a clan of poor but honest vagabonds and manages to outwit a band of city-slicker bureaucrats.

Kid Galahad
(United Artists, 1962) 95 min.

CREDITS: A Mirisch Company Production. Producer, David Weisbart; director, Phil Karlson; screenplay, William Fay; based on a story by Francis Wallace; photography, Burnett Guffey; music, Jeff Alexander; art direction, Cary Odell; set decoration, Edward G. Boyle; special effects, Milt Rice; costumes, Bert Henrikson and Irene Caine; assistant director, Jerome M. Siegel; editor, Stuart Gilmore. De Luxe Color.

CAST: Elvis Presley (Walter Gulick), Gig Young (Willy Grogan), Lola Albright (Dolly Fletcher), Joan Blackman (Rose Grogan), Charles Bronson (Lew Nyack), Ned Glass (Lieberman), Robert Emhardt (Maynard), David Lewis (Otto Danzig), Michael Dante (Joie Shakes), Judson Pratt (Zimmerman), George Mitchell (Sperling), Richard Devon (Marvin), Tommy Hart (Referee), Chris Alcaide (Henchman), Liam Redmond (Father Higgins), Jeffrey Morris (Ralphie), Roy Roberts (Promoter), Ralph Moody (Pete Prohosko), Ramon De La Fuente (Ramon "Sugar Boy" Romero), Frank Gerstle (Romero's Manager), George J. Lewis (Romero's Trainer).

SYNOPSIS: Elvis (in the old Wayne Morris role) is the likable country boy whom Gig Young attempts to turn into a boxing champ.

Girls! Girls! Girls!
(Paramount, 1962) 106 min.

CREDITS: A Hal Wallis Production. Producer, Hal B. Wallis; associate producer, Paul Nathan; director, Norman Taurog; screenplay, Allan Weiss and Edward Anhalt; based on a story by Weiss; photography, Loyal Griggs; music, Joseph J. Lilley; choreography, Charles O'Curran; art direction, Hal Pereira and Walter Tyler; set decoration, Sam Comer and Frank R. McKelvy; costumes, Edith Head; assistant director, D. Michael Moore; editor, Warren Low. Technicolor.

CAST: Elvis Presley (Ross Carpenter), Stella Stevens (Robin Gantner), Laurel Goodwin (Laurel Dodge), Jeremy Slate (Wesley Johnson), Robert Strauss (Sam), Frank Puglia (Alexander Stavros), Ginny Tiu (Mai Ling), Elizabeth Tiu (Tai Ling), Guy Lee (Chen Yung), Benson Fong (Kin Yung), Beulah Quo (Mme. Yung), Lili Valenty (Mama Stavros), Nestor Paiva (Arthur Morgan), Ann McCrea (Mrs. Morgan), Barbara Beall (Leona Stavros), Betty Beall (Linda Stavros), Gavin Gordon (Mr. Peabody), Mary Treen (Mrs. Figgor), Marjorie Bennett (Mrs. Dick), Kenneth Becker (Drunk), Richard Collier (Clerk).

SYNOPSIS: Nightclub singer Elvis loves his fishing boat more than the scads of girls who chase after him. However, wealthy Goodwin, who acquires his boat, also wins his heart, despite the competition of vocalist Stevens.

It Happened at the World's Fair
(Metro-Goldwyn-Mayer, 1963) 105 min.

CREDITS: Producer, Ted Richmond; director, Norman Taurog; screenplay, Si Rose and Seamon Jacobs; photography, Joseph Ruttenberg; music, Leith Stevens; choreography, Jack Baker; art direction, George W. Davis and Preston Ames; set decoration, Henry Grace and Hugh Hunt; technical advisor, Col. Tom Parker; assistant director, Al Jennings; editor, Fredric Steinkamp. Panavision and MetroColor. (Filmed on location at the Seattle World's Fair.)

CAST: Elvis Presley (Mike Edwards), Joan O'Brien (Diane Warren), Gary Lockwood (Danny Burke), Vicky Tiu (Sue-Lin), H. M. Wynant (Vince Bradley), Edith Atwater (Miss Steuben), Guy Raymond (Barney Thatcher), Dorothy Green (Miss Ettinger), Kam Tong (Walter Ling), Yvonne Craig (Dorothy Johnson), Russell Thorson (Sheriff), Wilson Wood (Mechanic), Robert B. Williams (Foreman), Olan Soule (Mr. Johnson), Jacqueline DeWit (Mrs. Johnson), John Day (Charlie), Robert "Red" West (Fred), Sandra Giles (June), Evelyn Dutton (Rita), Linda Humble (Redhead), Kurt Russell (Boy), The Jordanaires (Themselves), The Mello Men (Themselves).

SYNOPSIS: Elvis is a lothario/bush pilot who is grounded with his poker-playing sidekick (Lockwood), when a local sheriff attaches their plane as security for unpaid bills. Hitching a ride to Seattle, the two become involved with a Chinese farmer and his little girl.

Fun in Acapulco
(Paramount, 1963) 98 min.

CREDITS: A Hal Wallis Production. Producer, Hal B. Wallis; associate producer, Paul Nathan; director, Richard Thorpe; screenplay, Allan Weiss; photography, Daniel L. Fapp; music, Joseph J. Lilley; choreography, Charles O'Curran; art direction, Hal Pereira and Walter Tyler; set decoration, Sam Comer and Robert Benton; special effects, Paul K. Lerpae; costumes, Edith Head; technical advisor, Col. Tom Parker; 2nd unit and assistant director, Michael Moore; editor, Warren Low. Technicolor. (Filmed in Acapulco.)

CAST: Elvis Presley (Mike Windgren), Ursula Andress (Maggie Dauphine), Elsa Cardenas (Dolores Gomez), Paul Lukas (Maximilian), Larry Domasin (Raúl Almeido), Alejandro Rey (Moreno), Robert Carricart (José), Teri Hope (Janie Harkins), Charles Evans (Mr. Harkins), Howard McNear (Dr. John Stevers), Mary Treen (Mrs. Stevers), Alberto Morin (Hotel Manager), Francisco Ortega (Desk Clerk), Robert De Anda (Bellboy), Linda Rivera (Telegraph Clerk), Darlene Tomkins (First Girl), Linda Rand

(Second Girl), Adele Palacios (Secretary), The Jordanaires (Themselves), The Four Amigos (Themselves).

SYNOPSIS: Elvis is a hotel lifeguard/troubadour, haunted by a circus-trapeze accident back in the States.

Kissin' Cousins
(Metro-Goldwyn-Mayer, 1964) 96 min.

CREDITS: A Four Leaf Production. Producer, Sam Katzman; director, Gene Nelson; screenplay, Gerald Drayson Adams and Gene Nelson; based on a story by Adams; photography, Ellis W. Carter; music, Fred Karger; choreography, Hal Belfer; art direction, George W. Davis and Eddie Imazu; set decoration, Henry Grace and Budd S. Friend; technical advisor, Col. Tom Parker; assistant director, Eli Dunn; editor, Ben Lewis. Panavision and MetroColor.

CAST: Elvis Presley (Josh Morgan/Jodie Tatum), Arthur O'Connell (Pappy Tatum), Glenda Farrell (Ma Tatum), Jack Albertson (Capt. Robert Salbo), Pam Austin (Selena Tatum), Cynthia Pepper (Midge), Yvonne Craig (Azalea Tatum), Donald Woods (Gen. Alvin Danford), Tommy Farrell (M/Sgt. William George Bailey), Beverly Powers (Trudy), Hortense Petra (Dixie), Robert Stone (General's Aide), Joseph Esposito (Mike), Maureen Reagan (Lorraine), Joan Staley (Jonesy), Robert Carson (Gen. Sam Kruger).

SYNOPSIS: Elvis has two roles: an Air Force officer assigned to run a hillbilly family off its land so that the government can build a missile base; and (his color) the rambunctious spokesman/son of the hillfolk clan.

Viva Las Vegas
(Metro-Goldwyn-Mayer, 1964) 83 min.

CREDITS: Producers, Jack Cummings and George Sidney; director, George Sidney; screenplay, Sally Benson; photography, Joseph Biroc; music, George Stoll; choreography, David Winters; art direction, George W. Davis and Edward Carfagno; set decoration, Henry Grace and George R. Nelson; costumes, Don Feld; assistant director, Milton Feldman; editor, John McSweeney, Jr. Panavision and MetroColor. (British title: *Love in Las Vegas.*)

CAST: Elvis Presley (Lucky Jackson), Ann-Margret (Rusty Martin), Cesare Danova (Count Elmo Mancini), William Demarest (Mr. Martin), Nicky Blair (Shorty Farnsworth), Jack Carter (Himself), Robert B. Williams (Swanson), Bab Nash (Big Gus Olson), Roy Engel (Baker), Ford Dunhill (Driver), Barnaby Hale (Mechanic), Ivan Triesault (Head Captain), Eddie Quillan (M.C.), Francis Raval (Francois), Rick Murray (Delivery Boy), Larry Kent (Race Official), Howard Curtis (Starter), Alan Fordney (Race Announcer).

SYNOPSIS: Elvis plays a racedriving gambler out to win the Las Vegas Grand Prix.

Roustabout
(Paramount, 1964) 101 min.

CREDITS: A Hal Wallis Production. Producer, Hal B. Wallis; associate producer, Paul Nathan; director, John Rich; screenplay, Allan Weiss and Anthony Lawrence; based on a story by Weiss; photography, Lucien Ballard; music, Joseph J. Lilley; choreography, Earl Barton; art direction, Hal Pereira and Walter Tyler; set decoration, Sam Comer and Robert Benton; special effects, Paul K. Lerpae; costumes, Edith Head; technical advisor, Col. Tom Parker; assistant director, Michael Moore; editor, Warren Low. Techniscope and Technicolor.

CAST: Elvis Presley (Charlie Rogers), Barbara Stanwyck (Maggie Morgan), Joan Freeman (Cathy Lean), Leif Erickson (Joe Lean), Sue Ane Langdon (Mme. Mijanou), Pat Buttram (Harry Carver), Joan Staley (Marge), Dabbs Greer (Arthur Nielsen), Steve Brodie (Fred), Norman Grabowski (Sam), Jack Albertson (Lou), Jane Dulo (Hazel), Joel Fluellen (Cody Marsh), Arthur Levy (Gus), Toby Reed (Dick), Ray Kellogg (Ernie), Marianna Hill (Viola), Beverly Adams (Cora), Lester Miller (B.J.), Wilda Taylor (Little Egypt), Billy Barty (Bill the Midget), Raquel Welch (College Student), The Jordanaires (Themselves).

SYNOPSIS: Elvis is a footloose, guitar-playing motorcyclist who signs on with Barbara Stanwyck's small-time carnival.

Girl Happy
(Metro-Goldwyn-Mayer, 1965) 96 min.

CREDITS: A Euterpe Picture. Producer, Joe Pasternak; director, Boris Sagal; screenplay, Harvey Bullock and R. S. Allen; photography, Philip H. Lathrop; music, George Stoll; choreography, David Winters; art direction, George W. Davis and Addison Hehr; set decoration, Henry Grace and George R. Nelson; costumes, Don Feld; editor, Rita Roland. Panavision and MetroColor.

CAST: Elvis Presley (Rusty Wells), Shelley Fabares (Valerie), Harold J. Stone (Big Frank), Gary Crosby (Andy), Joby Baker (Wilbur), Nita Talbot (Sunny Daze), Mary Ann Mobley (Deena), Fabrizio Mioni (Romano), Jimmy Hawkins (Doc), Jackie Coogan (Sgt. Benson), Peter Brooks (Brentwood von Durgenfeld), John Fiedler (Mr. Penchill), Chris Noel (Betsy), Lyn Eddington (Laurie), Gale Gilmore (Nancy), Pamela Curran (Bobbie), Rusty Allen (Linda), Norman Grabowski ("Wolf Call" O'Brien), Mike de Anda (Bartender), Olan Soule (Waiter), Milton Frome (Police Captain), Beverly Adams (Girl), Jim Dawson (Muscle Boy), Ted Fish (Garbage Man), Dick Reeves (Officer Wilkins), Ralph Lee (Officer Jones), The Jordanaires (Themselves).

SYNOPSIS: Elvis is a combo leader hired by a tough Chicago nightclub owner (Stone) to keep an eye on his daughter (Fabares), romping in Fort Lauderdale with her college friends during the Easter vacation.

Tickle Me
(Allied Artists, 1965) 90 min.

CREDITS: Producer, Ben Schwalb; director, Norman Taurog; story and screenplay, Elwood Ullman and Edward Bernds; photography, Loyal Griggs; music, Walter Scharf; choreography, David Winters; art direction, Arthur Lonergan; set decoration, Arthur Krams; costumes, Leah Rhodes; assistant director, Artie Jacobson; editor, Archie Marshek. Panavision and De Luxe Color.

CAST: Elvis Presley (Lonnie Beale), Jocelyn Lane (Pam Merritt), Julie Adams (Vera Radford), Jack Mullaney (Stanley Potter), Merry Anders (Estelle Penfield), Connie Gilchrist (Hilda), Edward Faulkner (Brad Bentley), Bill Williams (Deputy Sturdivant), Louis Elias (Henry the Gardener), John Dennis (Adolph the Chef), Laurie Benton (Janet), Linda Rogers (Clair Kinnamon), Ann Morell (Sybyl), Lilyan Chauvin (Ronnie), Jean Ingram (Evelyn), Francine York (Mildred), Eve Bruce (Pat), Jackie Russell (Gloria), Angela Greene (Donna), Peggy Ward (Dot), Dorian Brown (Polly), Inez Pedroza (Ophelia), Grady Sutton (Mr. Dabney), Dorothy Conrad (Mrs. Dabney), Barbara Werle (Barbara), Allison Hayes (Mabel).

SYNOPSIS: Elvis is a singing bronco buster who takes a temporary job as a wrangler on an expensive dude ranch/beauty spa while awaiting the new rodeo season. (Note: *Tickle Me* opened in New York City less than one month after *Girl Happy*—which really was saturating the Presley market.)

Harum Scarum
(Metro-Goldwyn-Mayer, 1965) 84 min.

CREDITS: A Four Leaf Production. Producer, Sam Katzman; director, Gene Nelson; screenplay, Gerald Drayson Adams; photography, Fred H. Jackman; music, Fred Karger; choreography, Earl Barton; art direction, George W. Davis and H. McClure Capps; set decoration, Henry Grace and Don Greenwood, Jr.; technical advisor, Col. Tom Parker; assistant director, Eddie Saeta; editor, Ben Lewis. MetroColor. (Originally called *Harem Holiday* and *In My Harem*. British title: *Harem Holiday*.)

CAST: Elvis Presley (Johnny Tyronne), Mary Ann Mobley (Princess Shalimar), Fran Jeffries (Aishah), Michael Ansara (Prince Dragna), Jay Novello (Zacha), Philip Reed (King Toranshah), Theo Marcuse (Sinan), Billy Barty (Baba), Dirk Harvey (Mokar), Jack Costanzo (Julna), Larry Chance (Captain Herat), Barbara Werle (Leilah), Brenda Benet (Emerald), Gail Gilmore (Sapphire), Wilda Taylor (Amethyst), Vicki Malkin (Sari), Ryck Rydon (Mustapha), Richard Reeves (Scarred Bedouin), Joey Russo (Yussef), Suzanne Covington (Naja), Maja Stewart (Princess), Ralph Lee

(Noble), Robert Lamont (President), Hugh Sanders (Ambassador McCord), Judy Durell (Cashier).

SYNOPSIS: Elvis is a Hollywood star who gets involved in the machinations of a diabolical Arab sheik.

Frankie and Johnny
(United Artists, 1966) 87 min.

CREDITS: An Edward Small Production. Executive producer, Edward Small; director, Frederick De Cordova; associate producer and screenplay, Alex Gottlieb; story, Nat Perrin; photography, Jacques Marquette; music, Fred Karger; choreography, Earl Barton; art direction, Walter Simonds; set decoration, Morris Hoffman; costumes, Gwen Wakeling; editor, Grant Whytock. Technicolor.

CAST: Elvis Presley (Johnny), Donna Douglas (Frankie), Nancy Kovack (Nellie Bly), Sue Anne Langdon (Mitzi), Anthony Eisley (Clint Braden), Harry Morgan (Cully), Audrey Christie (Peg), Robert Strauss (Blackie), Jerome Cowan (Wilbur), The Earl Barton Dancers: Wilda Taylor, Larri Thomas, Dee Jay Mattis; Judy Chapman.

SYNOPSIS: Elvis is a riverboat gambler/singer in a period reworking of the traditional tale of American folklore.

Paradise-Hawaiian Style
(Paramount, 1966) 91 min.

CREDITS: A Hal Wallis Production. Producer, Hal B. Wallis; associate producer, Paul Nathan; director, Michael Moore; screenplay, Allan Weiss and Anthony Lawrence; story by Weiss; photography, W. Wallace Kelley; music, Joseph J. Lilley; choreography, Jack Regas; art direction, Hal Pereira and Walter Tyler; set decoration, Sam Comer and Ray Moyer; special effects, Romaine Birkmeyer; costumes, Edith Head; assistant director, James Rosenberger; editor, Warren Low. Technicolor. (Filmed in Hawaii.)

CAST: Elvis Presley (Rick Richards), Suzanna Leigh (Judy Hudson), James Shigeta (Danny Kohana), Donna Butterworth (Jan Kohana), Marianna Hill (Lani), Irene Tsu (Pua), Linda Wong (Lehua), Julie Parrish (Joanna), Jan Shepard (Betty Kohana), John Doucette (Donald Belden), Philip Ahn (Moki), Grady Sutton (Mr. Cubberson), Don Collier (Andy Lowell), Doris Packer (Mrs. Barrington), Mary Treen (Mrs. Belden), Gigi Verone (Peggy Holden).

SYNOPSIS: Elvis plays an ex-airline pilot gone native, hoping to start a charter helicopter service to fly tourists around the islands.

Spinout
(Metro-Goldwyn-Mayer, 1966) 93 min.

CREDITS: A Euterpe Picture. Producer, Joe Pasternak; associate producer, Hank Moonjean; director, Norman Taurog; screenplay, Theodore J. Flicker and George Kirgo; photography, Daniel L. Fapp; music, George Stoll; choreography, Jack Baker; art direction, George W. Davis and Edward Carfagno; set decoration, Henry Grace and Hugh Hunt; special visual effects, J. McMillan Johnson and Carroll L. Shepphird; technical advisor, Col. Tom Parker; assistant director, Claude Binyon, Jr.; editor, Rita Roland. Panavision and MetroColor. (British title: *California Holiday.*)

CAST: Elvis Presley (Mike McCoy), Shelley Fabares (Cynthia Foxhugh), Diane McBain (Diana St. Clair), Deborah Walley (Les), Dodie Marshall (Susan), Jack Mullaney (Curly), Will Hutchins (Lt. Tracy Richards), Warren Berlinger (Philip Short), Jimmy Hawkins (Larry), Carl Betz (Howard Foxhugh), Cecil Kellaway (Bernard Ranley), Una Merkel (Violet Ranley), Frederic Worlock (Blodgett), Dave Barry (Harry), The Jordanaires (Themselves).

SYNOPSIS: Elvis is a racedriver who prefers his Duesenberg to the willing dames.

Double Trouble
(Metro-Goldwyn-Mayer, 1967) 92 min.

CREDITS: Producers, Judd Bernard and Irwin Winkler; director, Norman Taurog; screenplay, Jo Heims; based on a story by Marc Brandel; photography, Daniel L. Fapp; music, Jeff Alexander; choreography, Alex Romero; art direction, George W. Davis and Merrill Pye; set decoration, Henry Grace and Hugh Hunt; special visual effects, J. McMillan Johnson and Carroll L. Shepphird; costumes, Don Feld; technical advisor, Col. Tom Parker; assistant director, Claude Binyon, Jr.; editor, John McSweeney. Panavision and MetroColor.

CAST: Elvis Presley (Guy Lambert), Annette Day (Jill Conway), John Williams (Gerald Waverly), Yvonne Romain (Claire Dunham), The Wiere Brothers (Themselves), Chips Rafferty (Archie Brown), Norman Rossington (Arthur Babcock), Monty Landis (Georgie), Michael Murphy (Morley), Leon Askin (Inspector De Grotte), John Alderson (Iceman), Stanley Adams (Capt. Roach), Maurice Marsac (Frenchman), Walter Burke (Mate), Helene Winston (Gerda), Monique Lemaire (Desk Clerk), The G Men (Themselves).

SYNOPSIS: Elvis is a discotheque singer who falls for an English heiress and becomes involved in mysterious doings by someone trying to impersonate him.

Easy Come, Easy Go
(Paramount, 1967) 97 min.

CREDITS: A Hal Wallis Production. Producer, Hal B. Wallis; associate producer, Paul Nathan; director, John Rich; screenplay, Allan Weiss and Anthony Lawrence; photography, William Margulies; music, Joseph J. Lilley; choreography, David Winters; art direction, Hal Pereira and Walter Tyler; set decoration, Robert Benton and Arthur Krams; underwater photography, Michael J. Dugan; special effects, Paul K. Lerpae; costumes, Edith Head; technical advisor, Col. Tom Parker; assistant director, Robert Goldstein; editor, Archie Marshek. Technicolor.

CAST: Elvis Presley (Ted Jackson), Dodie Marshall (Jo Symington), Pat Priest (Dina Bishop), Pat Harrington (Judd Whitman), Skip Ward (Gil Carey), Elsa Lanchester (Mme. Neherina), Frank McHugh (Captain Jack), Sandy Kenyon (Lt. Schwartz), Ed Griffith (Cooper), Read Morgan (Lt. Tompkins), Mickey Elley (Lt. Whitehead), Elaine Beckett (Vicki), Shari Nims (Mary), Diki Lerner (Zoltan), Kay York (Tanya), Robert Isenberg (Artist), The Jordanaires (Themselves).

SYNOPSIS: Elvis is an ex-frogman turned treasure hunter.

Clambake
(United Artists, 1967) 98 min.

CREDITS: Producers, Arnold Laven, Arthur Gardner, and Jules Levy; associate producer, Tom Rolf; director, Arthur H. Nadel; screenplay, Arthur Browne, Jr., based on his story; photography, William Margulies; music, Jeff Alexander; choreography, Alex Romero; art direction, Lloyd Papez; set decoration, James Red; special effects, Bob Warner; assistant director, Claude Binyon, Jr.; editor, Tom Rolf. Techniscope and Technicolor.

CAST: Elvis Presley (Scott Heyward), Shelley Fabares (Dianne Carter), Bill Bixby (James Jamison III), Will Hutchins (Tom Wilson), Gary Merrill (Sam Burton), James Gregory (Duster Heyward), Amanda Harley (Ellie), Suzie Kaye (Sally), Angelique Pettyjohn (Gloria), Olga Kaye (Gigi), Arlene Charles (Olive), Jack Good (Mr. Hathaway), Hal Peary (Doorman), Sam Riddle (Race Announcer), Sue England (Cigarette Girl), Liza Slagle (Lisa), Lee Krieger (Bartender), Herb Barnett (Waiter), Melvin Allen (Crewman), Steve Cory (Bellhop), Robert Lieb (Barasch), Red West (Ice Cream Vendor).

SYNOPSIS: Elvis is a millionaire's son who wants to make it on his own by becoming a speedboat racer.

Live a Little, Love a Little
(Metro-Goldwyn-Mayer, 1968) 89 min.

CREDITS: Producer, Douglas Laurence; director, Norman Taurog; screenplay,

Michael A. Hoey and Dan Greenburg; based on the novel *Kiss My Firm but Pliant Lips* by Greenburg; photography, Fred Koenekamp; music, Billy Strange; "Dream Sequence" choreographed by Jack Regas; "A Little Less Conversation" choreographed by Jack Baker; art direction, George W. Davis and Preston Ames; set decoration, Henry Grace and Don Greenwood, Jr.; assistant director, Al Shenberg; editor, John McSweeney; Panavision and MetroColor.

CAST: Elvis Presley (Greg), Michele Carey (Bernice), Don Porter (Mike Landsdown), Rudy Vallee (Penlow), Dick Sargent (Harry), Sterling Holloway (Milkman), Celeste Yarnell (Ellen), Eddie Hodges (Delivery Boy), Joan Shawlee (Robbie's Mother), Emily Banks (Receptionist), Michael Keller (Art Director), Merri Ashley (1st Secretary), Phyllis Davis (2nd Secretary), Ursula Menzel (Perfume Model), Susan Shute (Model No. 1), Edie Baskin (Model No. 2), Gabrielle (Model No. 3), Giny Kaneen (Model No. 4), Susan Henning (Mermaid), Morgan Windbell (1st Motorcycle Cop), Benjie Nacroft (2nd Motorcycle Cop).

SYNOPSIS: Elvis plays a fashion photographer kidnapped by a rich kook (Carey) and guarded by her monstrous Great Dane.

Speedway
(Metro-Goldwyn-Mayer, 1968) 94 min.

CREDITS: Producer, Douglas Laurence; director, Norman Taurog; screenplay, Phillip Shuken; photography, Joseph Ruttenberg; music, Jeff Alexander; art direction, George W. Davis and Leroy Coleman; set decoration, Henry Grace and Don Greenwood, Jr.; special visual effects, Carroll L. Shepphird; assistant director, Dale Hutchinson; editor, Richard Farrell. Panavision and MetroColor. (Filmed at Charlotte Speedway in North Carolina.)

CAST: Elvis Presley (Steve Grayson), Nancy Sinatra (Susan Jacks), Bill Bixby (Kenny Donford), Gale Gordon (R. W. Hepworth), William Schallert (Abel Esterlake), Victoria Meyerink (Ellie Esterlake), Ross Hagen (Paul Dado), Carl Ballentine (Birdie Kebner), Robert Harris (Lloyd Meadow), Michele Newman (Debbie Esterlake), Poncie Ponce (Juan Medala), Courtney Brown (Carrie Esterlake), Dana Brown (Billie Esterlake), Patti Jean Keith (Annie Esterlake), Harper Carter (Ted Simmons), Christopher West (Billie Jo), Carl Reindel (Mike), Harry Hickox (The Cook), Miss Beverly Hills (Mary Ann), Gari Hardy (Dumb Blonde), Charlotte Considine (Lori), Sandy Reed (Race Announcer), The Jordanaires (Themselves).

SYNOPSIS: Elvis is a stockcar racer who falls for the IRS agent (Sinatra) secretly investigating his finances.

Stay Away, Joe
(Metro-Goldwyn-Mayer, 1968) 101 min.

CREDITS: Producer, Douglas Laurence; director, Peter Tewksbury; screenplay, Burt

Kennedy and Michael A. Hoey; based on the novel by Dan Cushman; photography, Fred Koenekamp; music, Jack Marshall; art direction, George W. Davis and Carl Anderson; set decoration, Henry Grace and Don Greenwood, Jr.; assistant director, Dale Hutchinson; editor, George W. Brooks. Panavision and MetroColor. (Filmed in Sedona, Arizona.)

CAST: Elvis Presley (Joe Lightcloud), Burgess Meredith (Charlie Lightcloud), Joan Blondell (Glenda Callahan), Katy Jurado (Annie Lightcloud), Thomas Gomez (Grandpa), Henry Jones (Hy Slager), L. Q. Jones (Bronc Hoverty), Quentin Dean (Mamie Callahan), Anne Seymour (Mrs. Hawkins), Angus Duncan (Lorne Hawkins), Douglas Henderson (Congressman Morrissey), Michael Lane (Frank Hawk), Susan Trustman (Mary Lightcloud), Warren Vanders (Hike Bowers), Buck Kartalian (Bull Shortgun), Maurishka (Connie Shortgun), Caitlin Wyles (Marlene Standing Rattle), Marya Christen (Billie-Jo Hump), Del "Sonny" West (Jackson He-Crow), Jennifer Peak (Little Deer), Brett Parker (Dep. Sheriff Hank Matson), Michael Keller (Orville Witt), Dick Wilson (Salesman), David Cadiente (Indian), Harry Harvey, Sr. (Judge Nibley), Joe Esposito (Workman), Robert Lieb (Announcer), The Jordanaires (Themselves).

SYNOPSIS: Rodeo rider Elvis returns to the Cree Indian reservation to help his dad participate in a government rehabilitation scheme. Elvis's romances include attractive but dim-witted Dean, the daughter of the local restaurant owner.

Charro!
(National General Pictures, 1969) 98 min.

CREDITS: Executive producer, Harry Caplan; producer/director/writer, Charles Marquis Warren; based on a story by Frederic Louis Fox; photography, Ellsworth Fredericks; music, Hugo Montenegro; title song, Hugo Montenegro and Alan & Marilyn Bergman; art direction, James Sullivan; set decoration, Charles Thompson; special effects, George (Bud) Thompson, Woodrow Ward, and Robert Beck; associate producer and assistant director, Dink Templeton; editor, Al Clark. Technicolor and Panavision.

CAST: Elvis Presley (Jess Wade), Ina Balin (Tracy), Victor French (Vince), Barbara Werle (Sara Ramsey), Solomon Sturges (Billy Roy), Lynn Kellogg (Marcie), Paul Brinegar (Opie Keetch), James Sikking (Gunner), Harry Landers (Heff), Tony Young (Lt. Rivera), James Almanzar (Sheriff Ramsay), Charles H. Gray (Mody), Rodd Redwing (Lige), Gary Walberg (Martin Tilford), Duane Grey (Gabe), John Pickard (Jerome Selby), J. Edward McKinley (Henry Carter), Robert Luster (Will Joslyn), Christa Lang (Christa), Robert Karnes (Bartender).

SYNOPSIS: Reformed outlaw Elvis confronts his former gang in an American border town. He not only outmaneuvers the outlaws but he wins the love of Balin, owner of the local saloon.

The Trouble with Girls
(Metro-Goldwyn-Mayer, 1969) 104 min.

CREDITS: Producer, Lester Welch; associate producer, Wilson McCarthy; director, Peter Tewksbury; screenplay, Arnold & Lois Peyser; based on the novel *The Chautauqua* by Day Keene and Dwight Babcock and a story by Mauri Grashin; photography, Jacques Marquette; music, Billy Strange; choreography, Jonathan Lucas; art direction, George W. Davis and Edward Carfagno; set decoration, Henry Grace and Jack Mills; costumes, Bill Thomas; assistant director, John Clark Bowman; editor, George W. Brooks. MetroColor.

CAST: Elvis Presley (Walter Hale), Marlyn Mason (Charlene), Nicole Jaffe (Betty), Sheree North (Nita Bix), Edward Andrews (Johnny), John Carradine (Mr. Drewcolt), Vincent Price (Mr. Morality), Anissa Jones (Carol), Joyce Van Patten (Maude), Pepe Brown (Willy), Dabney Coleman (Harrison Wilby), Bill Zuckert (Mayor Gilchrist), Pitt Herbert (Mr. Perper), Anthony Teague (Clarence), Med Flory (Constable), Robert Nichols (Smith), Helene Winston (Olga Prchlik), Kevin O'Neal (Yale), Frank Welker (Rutgers), John Rubinstein (Princeton), Chuck Briles (Amherst), Patsy Garrett (Mrs. Gilchrist), Linda Sue Risk (Lily-Jeanne), Charles P. Thompson (Cabbie), Leonard Rumery (1st Farmhand), William M. Paris (2nd Farmhand), Kathleen Rainey (3rd Farmhand), Hal James Pederson (Soda Jerk), Mike Wagner (Chowderhead), Brett Parker (Iceman), Duke Snider (The Cranker), Pacific Palisades High School Madrigals (Choral Society).

SYNOPSIS: Elvis is the manager of a traveling chautauqua company of the 1920s.

Change of Habit
(Universal, 1969) 93 min.

CREDITS: Producer, Joe Connelly; associate producer, Irving Paley; director, William Graham; screenplay, James Lee & S. S. Schweitzer and Eric Bercovici; story, John Joseph and Richard Morris; photography, Russell Metty; music, Billy Goldenberg; songs, Ben Weisman and Buddy Kaye; art direction, Alexander Golitzen and Frank Arrigo; set decoration, John McCarthy and Ruby Levitt; costumes, Helen Colvig; assistant director, Phil Bowles; editor, Douglas Stewart. Technicolor.

CAST: Elvis Presley (Dr. John Carpenter), Mary Tyler Moore (Sister Michelle), Barbara McNair (Sister Irene), Jane Elliot (Sister Barbara), Leora Dana (Mother Joseph), Edward Asner (Lt. Moretti), Robert Emhardt (The Banker), Regis Toomey (Father Gibbons), Doro Merande (Rose), Ruth McDevitt (Lily), Richard Carlson (Bishop Finley), Nefti Millet (Julio Hernandez), Lorena Kirk (Angela), Laura Figueroa (Desiree), Virginia Vincent (Miss Parker), David Renard (Colom), Bill Elliott (Robbie), Rodolfo Hoyos (Mr. Hernandez), Ji-Tu Cumbuka (Hawk).

SYNOPSIS: Elvis is a "street" doctor in the ghetto who falls for one of his assistants, unaware that she is actually a nun on temporary outside assignment.

Elvis...That's the Way It Is
(Metro-Goldwyn-Mayer, 1970) 108 min.

CREDITS: Producer, Herbert F. Soklow; director, Denis Sanders; written by Denis Sanders; photography, Lucien Ballard; music conductor, Joe Guercio; Elvis's wardrobe, Bill Belew; technical advisor, Col. Tom Parker; assistant director, John Wilson; editor, Henry Berman. Panavision and MetroColor.

CAST: Elvis Presley, James Burton, Charlie Hodge, Ronnie Tutt, Glen Hardin, Jerry Scheff, John Wilkinson, Millie Kirkham, The Imperials, The Sweet Inspirations, and unbilled guest appearances by Cary Grant, Sammy Davis, Jr., Juliet Prowse, Dale Robertson, Xavier Cugat, Charo, Norm Crosby.

SYNOPSIS: Beginning with rehearsals at the MGM studios, the documentary traces Elvis's preparations for his first concert tour since 1957, and moves onward to Las Vegas, where his summer festival begins.

Elvis on Tour
(Metro-Goldwyn-Mayer, 1972) 93 min.

CREDITS: Produced, directed, and written by Pierre Adidge and Robert Abel; associate producer, Sidney Levin; photography, Robert E. Thomas; music conductor, Joe Guercio; montage supervisor, Martin Scorsese; Elvis's wardrobe, Bill Belew; technical advisor, Col. Tom Parker; assistant director, Ephraim "Red" Schaffer; editor, Ken Zemke. MetroColor.

CAST: Elvis Presley, Vernon Presley, Jackie Kahane, James Burton, Charlie Hodge, Ronnie Tutt, Glen Hardin, Jerry Scheff, John Wilkinson, Kathy Westmoreland, J. D. Sumner, The Stamps Quartet, The Sweet Inspirations.

SYNOPSIS: A cinema-verité documentary of Elvis's 1972 concert tour, combined with film highlights from his career, including clips from his early Ed Sullivan appearances and scenes from his MGM and Hal B. Wallis movies.

Elvis Presley's Television Appearances

STAGE SHOW with Tommy and
Jimmy Dorsey (CBS)

January 28, 1956
February 4, 1956
February 11, 1956
February 18, 1956
March 17, 1956
March 24, 1956

THE MILTON BERLE SHOW (NBC)

April 3, 1956
June 5, 1956

THE STEVE ALLEN SHOW (NBC)

July 1, 1956

ED SULLIVAN'S TOAST OF THE TOWN (CBS)

September 9, 1956
October 28, 1956
January 6, 1957

THE TODAY SHOW (NBC)

*Excerpt from Elvis's press
conference at Fort Dix, New Jersey,
on completion of his U.S.
Army tour of duty: March 4, 1960*

THE FRANK SINATRA TIMEX SHOW (ABC)

May 12, 1960

SINGER PRESENTS ELVIS (NBC)

December 3, 1968

ELVIS: ALOHA FROM HAWAII (NBC)

April 4, 1973

Elvis Presley's Club Appearances

FRONTIER HOTEL, LAS VEGAS

March 23–29, 1956

INTERNATIONAL HOTEL, LAS VEGAS

July 31–August 28, 1969
January 26–February 23, 1970
August 30–September 7, 1970
January 26–February 23, 1971
August 9–September 6, 1971
January 26–February 23, 1972
August 4–September 4, 1972

SAHARA TAHOE, LAKE TAHOE

July 20–August 2, 1971
May 4–20, 1973
May 16–26, 1974
October 11–14, 1974
April 30–May 9, 1976

LAS VEGAS HILTON, LAS VEGAS

January 26–February 23, 1973
August 6–September 3, 1973
January 26–February 9, 1974
August 20–September 2, 1974
March 18–31, 1975
August 18–September 2, 1975
December 2–15, 1975
August 20–September 1, 1976
    (canceled after three nights due to illness)
December 1–12, 1976

Elvis Presley's Concert Tours

1970

February 27– March 1	Livestock Show, Houston
September 9	Phoenix
September 10	St. Louis
September 11	Detroit
September 12	Miami
September 13	Tampa
September 14	Mobile
November 10	Oakland
November 11	Portland, Ore.
November 12	Seattle
November 13	San Francisco
November 14	Los Angeles
November 15	San Diego
November 16	Oklahoma City
November 17	Denver

1971

November 5	Minneapolis
November 6	Cleveland
November 7	Louisville
November 8	Philadelphia
November 9	Baltimore
November 10	Boston
November 11	Cincinnati
November 12	Houston
November 13	Dallas
November 14	Tuscaloosa
November 15	Kansas City
November 16	Salt Lake City

1972

April 5	Buffalo
April 6	Detroit
April 7	Dayton
April 8	Knoxville
April 9	Hampton Roads
April 10	Richmond
April 11	Roanoke
April 12	Indianapolis
April 13	Charlotte
April 14	Greensboro
April 15	Macon
April 16	Jacksonville
April 17	Little Rock
April 18	San Antonio
April 19	Albuquerque
June 9–11	New York City, Madison Square Garden
June 12	Fort Wayne
June 13	Evansville
June 14–15	Milwaukee
June 16–17	Chicago
June 18	Fort Worth
June 19	Wichita
June 20	Tulsa
November 8	Lubbock
November 9	Tucson
November 10	El Paso
November 11	Oakland
November 12–13	San Bernardino
November 14–15	Long Beach
November 17–18	Honolulu

1973

January 14	Honolulu, Worldwide Satellite Show, Honolulu International Center
June 20	Mobile
June 21	Atlanta
June 22–24	Uniondale, Nassau Memorial Coliseum
June 25–26	Pittsburgh
June 27	Cincinnati
June 28	St. Louis
June 29–30	Atlanta
July 1	Nashville
July 2	Oklahoma City

1974

June 15–16	Fort Worth
June 17-18	Baton Rouge
June 19	Amarillo
June 20	Des Moines
June 21	Cleveland
June 22	Providence
June 23	Philadelphia
June 24	Niagara Falls
June 25	Columbus
June 26	Louisville
June 27	Bloomington
June 28	Milwaukee
June 29	Kansas City
June 30– July 1	Omaha
July 2	Salt Lake City

1975

March 19	Charlotte
March 20	Johnson City
March 21	Cincinnati
April 24	Macon
April 25	Jacksonville
April 26	Tampa
April 27–28	Lakeland
April 29	Murfreesboro
April 30– May 2	Atlanta
May 3	Monroe
May 4	Lake Charles
May 5	Jackson
May 6–7	Murfreesboro
May 30– June 1	Huntsville
June 2	Mobile
June 3	Tuscaloosa
June 4–5	Houston
June 6	Dallas
June 7	Shreveport
June 8–9	Jackson
June 10	Memphis
July 10	Cleveland
July 11	Charleston
July 12	Niagara Falls
July 14–15	Springfield
July 16	New Haven
July 18	Cleveland
July 19	Uniondale
July 20	Norfolk
July 22	Asheville, N.C.
December 31	Detroit (Presley earned $816,000 in one performance, believed to be the all-time record for a single performer anywhere.)

1976

April 21	Kansas City
April 22	Omaha
April 23	Denver
April 24	San Diego
April 26	Long Beach
April 28	Seattle
April 29	Spokane
June 24	Syracuse
June 25	Buffalo
June 26	Rochester
June 27	Syracuse
July 4	Memphis
July 24	Charleston
July 26	Landover
July 27	Providence
July 28	Hartford
July 29	Springfield
July 30	New Haven
August 7–8	Syracuse
August 31	Macon
September 4	Lakeland
October 14–15	Chicago
October 16	Duluth
October 17	Minneapolis
October 18	Sioux Falls
October 19	Madison
October 20	South Bend
October 21	Kalamazoo
October 22	Urbana, University of Illinois
October 23	Cleveland
November 28	Anaheim
November 29	San Francisco
December 28	Dallas
December 30	Birmingham

1977

March 23	Tempe, University of Arizona
March 24	Amarillo
March 25–26	Norman
April 20	Columbia
April 21	Greensboro
April 22	Detroit
April 23	Toledo
April 24	Saginaw
April 27	Milwaukee
April 30	St. Paul
May 22	Landover
May 23	Providence
May 24	Augusta
May 25	Rochester
May 26–27	Birmingham
May 28	Philadelphia
May 29	Baltimore (Presley walked out on his audience for the first time in career.)
June 2	Mobile
June 18	Kansas City
June 25	Cincinnati

Tour canceled due to death:

August 17-18	Portland, Me.
August 19	Utica
August 20	Syracuse
August 21	Hartford
August 22	Uniondale
August 23	Lexington
August 24	Roanoke
August 25	Fayetteville
August 26	Ashville, N.Y.
August 27–28	Memphis